The Optimistic Pessimist

More Timeless Ideas

Moshe Cohen

Copyright © 2023 by Moshe Cohen

All rights reserved. No part of this publication may be reproduced, distributed, or transmitted in any form or by any means, including photocopying, recording, or other electronic or mechanical methods, without the prior written permission of the publisher, except in the case of brief quotations embodied in critical reviews and certain other noncommercial uses permitted by copyright law.

ISBN: 978-1-7352600-4-4 (paperback)
ISBN: 978-1- 7352600-5-1 (ebook)
Library of Congress Control Number: 2023915617

Front cover design by Harini Rajagopalan.
Front cover icon by Brand Mania from The Noun Project.
Book design by Harini Rajagopalan.
www.harini-rajagopalan.squarespace.com

First printing edition 2023.

The Negotiating Table, Inc.
1089, Commonwealth Avenue #354
Boston, MA 02115
www.neotiatingtable.com

The Optimistic Pessimist

Acknowledgments

There are, as always more people to acknowledge than I can list. First, I would like to acknowledge my mother, Aviva Wertheim Cohen, who taught me optimism through personal example. Although gone for nearly twenty years, her voice, face and lessons are etched in my soul. Without her, I might never have learned to be an optimistic pessimist.

Similarly, from my grandparents, Miriam and Haim Wertheim, and Bracha and Zecharia Cohen, I learned that we all have choices, and that sometimes the longer, more difficult route turns out to be the best. I'm blessed with a large and close extended family of uncles, aunts, cousins, and more, from whom I have drawn support and inspiration.

I'm grateful to my wife, Barbra Batshalom, my wonderful children, Maya, Ariel, Elan, and Nadav, and my sister, Iris Cohen Fineberg for providing me with support in all my endeavors and teaching me so much about the world. I'm also thankful to Skye Annica and Catie Hutchings, for demonstrating the power of mindfulness and love.

A huge thank you to Ryan Orr, who once again edited my manuscript with a keen eye and thoughtful feedback, and to Harini Rajagopalan, for designing the appearance of the book, inside and out.

As always, thanks to the many teachers, colleagues, family members, friends, clients, and especially students, from whom I learn every day and who foster the environment in which these ideas sprouted and grew. I'm grateful to have learned from you.

But, at this moment in time, I'd like to dedicate this book to my father, Hanania Cohen, whose wisdom, guidance, companionship, struggles, and journey have accompanied me for over six decades. Even as the setting sun ushers in the darkness of night, we bask in a beautiful sunset, reminding us once again to appreciate every moment and focus on the positive. Our journey together has taught me that optimism is more than a choice, habit, or even lifestyle, but instead a necessity if we are to truly live our lives. I love you so much! You are in my mind every day.

Contents

Acknowledgments	3
Introduction	9
The Optimistic Pessimist	12
A Whale Story	14
People are Annoying!	16
Alone, but Okay with It	18
Choices	20
Not All Bad	22
Angry Earth	24
Summer Infestations	26
Ordinary Extraordinary	28
Worlds Gone By	30
What Are We Made Of?	32
Irrational Fears	34
The Year of the Introvert	36
Lest We Forget	38
The Meaning of Life	40
When Will It End?	42
Everything is Temporary	44
Out of Control	46

Time is Finite	48
Beyond Alternative Facts	50
Outrage and Empathy	52
Bummer, Bumper, Bumpy	54
No Plans or Goals	56
Comfort in the Mundane	58
Learning Greek	60
Angry	62
The Small Stuff	64
De-Graded	66
The Day After	68
Done with Covid	70
Nothing is Real	72
Beyond the Red Giant	74
Hot and Cold	76
The Blizzard of 2022	78
Moving On	80
The Great Reset	82
Invisible Anxiety	84
Henchmen	86
Cousins	88
The Rear-View Mirror	90

Normal but Weird	92
Yes or No?	94
Inflation	96
Optimism and the End of Humanity	98
What Do We Know?	100
The Passage of Time	102
Never Good Enough	104
Where to Begin	106
Ripples	108
A Quiet Day	110
Money	112
Up, Up and Away	114
The Tides	116
Not So Simple	118
The Bystander Effect	120
Lies and Illusions	122
Feeling the Heat	124
Always Negotiating	126
The Sandcastle	128
Go Away!	130
The Return of Spontaneity	132
Back to Normal	134

Pessimism is a Luxury	136
Endings	138
Concluding Thoughts	140

Introduction

In March of 2020, the world shut down due to the Covid-19 pandemic, and to help myself and those around me muddle through it, I started writing and posting short essays on optimism and other topics. When the lockdown ended, over a year later, I compiled these essays into a volume called *Optimism is a Choice and Other Timeless Ideas*. But, while the lockdown ended, the pandemic hadn't, so I kept writing and posting essays.

Now, nearly two years later, it seems that this pandemic is finally behind us, or at least less defining of our lives. While it hasn't gone away, and people are still getting sick, other matters have taken over our attention. We are worried about inflation, politics, war, and even the flu way more than we are about Covid-19. The pandemic is becoming endemic, and we are learning to live with it.

Therefore, it is time to conclude this series of essays, and to mark this transition, I've put together this second volume of essays, called *The Optimistic Pessimist*. All in all, the 61 essays in the first volume and the 64 essays in the second form both a pandemic diary, tracing the arc of the past two and a half years, and some philosophical advice, rooted in the idea that we create our own experience through our attitude and approach to life.

If I've learned anything over the past few years it is that we control very little of what happens to us, but we do have a say in how we think about things. By becoming more mindful and deliberate in our choices, we can give ourselves a positive life experience even through unfavorable circumstances. We can notice the small wonders around us, emphasize the good things, and stay hopeful, even as we recognize the complex and often difficulty reality surrounding us.

Optimism is a choice, and not always an easy choice. While my temperament is often anxious and my mind naturally creates fear-based pessimistic narratives, I have chosen to be optimistic and positive as my go-to response to the world. My experience is defined by gratitude, and I feel very lucky. For me, optimism is a choice that started with a decision, turned into a routine, followed by a habit, and then a practice, and finally, a way of life.

Along the way, I've interacted with many students, colleagues, clients, and friends, and shared my enthusiasm for positivity and joy. I've enjoyed seeing the uplifting impact on their lives, and I hope that this collection of essays helps you as well.

Chapter 1

The Optimistic Pessimist

June 5

> *The universe amazes me, and I love gazing at the night sky, though I don't look for my fate in the stars, but instead in my choices. What happens, happens. That's not up to me. My attitude is!*

Outwardly, I am a relentless optimist, focused on the positive, looking for opportunities, and encouraging those around me to believe in possibilities rather than problems. I believe I will find parking, and generally do. I expect traffic lights to turn green when I arrive, and they often oblige. I arrive at the airport twenty-five minutes before my flight and still make it onto the plane.

Around others, I'm even more of an optimist, supporting and encouraging people's efforts and helping them imagine good outcomes around the corner. I help them persevere through setbacks and challenges and carry them over the finish line when they falter. I remind them that even when everything looks cloudy and grey, the sun is shining above the clouds, and tomorrow, a new day will dawn. I support people both in my personal and in my professional life and try to help them be more positive.

But alone, in the dark, when the commotion has died down, I retreat into my mind and struggle with worry and anxiety, imagining catastrophic scenarios and anticipating myriad ways in which things could go wrong. At times, I'm grumpy and unpleasant, muttering negative commentary to myself. I get sad, depressed, disheartened, and discouraged and often feel lonely, even around the people I love most. When I stop paying attention and let my emotions drift of their own accord, I can be quite the pessimist.

My optimism is therefore not a product of my natural inclination but is instead an intentional practice that I've adopted and turned into a life habit. Somewhere along the way, I understood that my quality of life is determined partly by my genetic makeup, even more by my environment, but mostly by my choices. On one level, I am who I am. My DNA determines what I look like, how tall I am, and how my brain is constructed. Perhaps my brain has more anxious and sad neurons than is ideal, but that is the hand I've been dealt, and I don't control my genetics.

The environment in which I grew up also influenced my mental, social, and emotional well-being, and as a child, I had little say over my surroundings. My family, schools, neighborhood, and society influenced what I did, how I felt, and how I interacted with others. As I grew older, I did make decisions that helped me shape, though not entirely control my environment. I choose where to live, who to spend time with, what work to do, what to buy, and how to spend my time, and these choices impact my quality of life.

Over time, I've come to realize that the only thing I really control is my attitude, and that despite my natural tendencies, I can choose to be positive. Confronted by any circumstance, I must decide where to focus and what to emphasize. For me, optimism is a conscious choice, requiring effort and persistence. It has become my way of life, and I'm very grateful.

Chapter 2

A Whale Story

June 12

> *The world is a hilarious place, if you have laughter in your heart, and when you learn to find the funny bits in everything around you, joy and mirth will follow.*

I love hearing about things that I couldn't possibly make up, like the story of a Cape Cod lobster diver who was swallowed whole by a humpback whale and kept in its mouth for just under a minute before it spat him out at the surface. Imagine this from the whale's point of view: It's the equivalent for us opening our mouth to take in a Tic Tac and instead closing our jaws around a live rat that tastes all wrong and wriggles in our mouth, too big to swallow and just plain disgusting. No wonder the whale spat him out, and it probably would have done so sooner had it not been underwater at the time and needed to go up to breathe. I wonder how much krill the whale had to eat after in order to get the taste of diver out of its mouth.

From the diver's point of view, this wasn't a fun experience either, though things could have ended up a lot worse. To me, this story first illustrates the importance of luck. The diver was lucky to be alive, the whale was lucky to have been able to spit out the diver without getting him caught in its throat, and the krill were lucky to have escaped their fate, at least for a little while. Luck plays such an important role in what happens to us, and every time we achieve something through our prowess or skill, we should remember this story and the lesson that skill and smarts matter, but so does luck.

It's also helpful to complement luck with a whole lot of gratitude. If this were us, we might feel gratitude for having not been crushed by the whale's jaws, for the diving gear continuing to work inside the whale's mouth, for the relatively short duration before the whale spat us out, for not getting an embolism, for help being nearby, and more. It's easy to get caught up in the negatives, but this is at its core a very positive story, for which we should be grateful.

Another great lesson is one of perspective-taking. We are human, and the story was told to us by another human, so naturally, we first think of what happened in terms of the impact on the diver. But, if we can flip our minds around and think of this story from the whale's point of view, or even the krill's, then our experience and understanding of the world around us is enriched. So, reality is a great teacher once again, if only we open our minds to its lessons, and in the process, have a good laugh at the improbable absurdity of the story.

Chapter 3

People are Annoying!

June 19

> *We can enjoy time with nearly anyone, so long as its's not too much time. If we can keep our interactions with people each to the right dosage, we can have fun in almost any circumstance.*

People are annoying! They are also wonderful and amazing, but I'll save those thoughts for a different time. Today, I want to focus on the coworker who sits near you and hums without realizing you can hear them, the person who talks on the phone too loud or who leaves food wrappers on the breakroom counter, the one who interrupts you when you're trying to think, or who clips their fingernails at their desk. Sometimes what they are doing isn't bad, but it's still annoying – they might type too loud or breathe heavily, might have an irritating laugh or a distracting sniffle. Let's face it, we are annoying! I am, you are, we all are, and the closer we are physically, the more time we spend together, the more annoying we become. There's no getting away from it.

Except, for the past year and a half, there has been. We have been working remotely, far away from all of the other annoying people at the office, and connecting only by Zoom, phone, email, and other electronic means. Of course, being virtual has had its drawbacks, and we do miss the interaction, but on the other hand, being far away has given us control.

We can talk and engage with people when we need or want to, but then we can turn them off. We don't need to hear their noises when we want our quiet time, we can avoid smelling them, or seeing them, or observing their habits. They can't interrupt us in the same way, we don't have to pick up after their messes, and we aren't subjected to their annoying quirks every minute of the day, week after week. In a way, it's blissful.

Going remote was very difficult for many people and organizations. How do we make up for the lost informal interactions? How do we manage feelings of loneliness and isolation? How do we create and maintain a common culture when people hardly ever see each other? How can we become friends with people we never really meet? While working from home has been convenient for some people, it has also been very challenging for others, and the pandemic restrictions have forced many organizations to rethink and adjust how they operate.

Now, as many companies are returning to the office, there will be joy in this for many, but also challenges. After a year in which only our dog chewed with its mouth open, tolerating our coworker's sandwich might be hard to get used to. After shutting our coworkers, bosses, and reports on and off at will, it might be hard to adjust to a new world in which they are in our faces, ears and noses. To ensure a positive reentry, we, as organizations and individuals need to approach each other with tolerance and empathy, knowing that we are just as likely to be annoying to those around us as they are to us.

Chapter 4

Alone, but Okay with It

June 26

> *Carl Sagan said that "astronomy is a humbling and character-building experience." Gazing up at the stars helps us see how small we are in the vastness of it all, and this realization is very healthy for us.*

During the pandemic, many of us were alone more than we had been in a long time. We were confined to our homes due to lockdowns, banished from our places of work, shuttered out of stores and restaurants, and isolated from our family and friends. For some of us, the solitude was a welcome respite, for others, agonizing separation, and for many, a little bit of both.

We are a social species, and living apart from others is difficult for us. On the other hand, we are a paranoid, vengeful, and territorial species, afraid that others will overpower us and take away our lands, possessions, and control. This is why we prepare for war with other people, and why we dominate the natural world around us, driving rival species to extinction. It's also true as we look beyond our planet and speculate about the existence of extraterrestrial beings.

The U.S. government recently released its report on UFOs, also known as unidentified aerial phenomena, or UAPs. While the report details over one hundred sightings of these objects, it seemed no closer to verifying whether they are flying saucers packed with extraterrestrial visitors or merely unexplained Earthly phenomena. Some people may have been disappointed by this report, hoping to hear of massive cover-ups and definitive proof of aliens visiting from space. Others might have been disappointed in the other direction, hoping to finally see science debunk the idea that aliens exist.

The report is unlikely to change anyone's opinion. Those who believe that aliens have visited us on Earth are not going to be deterred by a lack of conclusive evidence. They are unwilling to accept the notion that we are alone, even as they fear an alien takeover of our planet. After all, the aliens, as portrayed in movies and in the UFO community range from benign and friendly to hostile and destructive. Perhaps it's not the aliens we see, but the ones we fear or so desperately want to see that drive our beliefs. First, we believe, and then we interpret the images to match our beliefs.

Carl Sagan spoke of this extensively in *The Demon-Haunted World*, where he showed that without learning how to think like scientists, we lose the ability to differentiate between fact and fiction and are therefore at the mercy of our imaginations and the fanciful explanations presented to us by others. People sometimes confuse science with knowing facts, but scientific thinking is actually about not knowing, being skeptical about anything until we can prove it beyond reasonable doubt.

Are we the only ones? If other intelligent beings exist, will we ever make contact? Who knows! The universe is vast, and for now, we can only keep looking. Until there's proof, we remain must resign ourselves to isolation with each other upon this small, fragile planet we call home. Perhaps someday this might change, but until then, we are alone, and I, for one, am okay with that.

Chapter 5

Choices

July 4

> *Making decisions is often hard and sometimes painful. Not making decisions is worse, as we live in denial and suffer from anxiety. In the end, something happens anyway.*

Every day, we are confronted with choices, whether we are aware of them or not.

Some choices are consequential, while other choices seem important at the time, but ultimately don't matter much. The process we use to make these decisions is largely intuitive and emotionally driven, and for many, involves some degree of anxiety. We avoid and procrastinate, research and over-think, agonize over our options, and end up choosing poorly, or not at all.

Some decisions involve major life choices – should we get married, move, change jobs, have children, buy a house, go back to school, retire, divorce our spouse, have surgery? We are often so overwhelmed by these choices that we postpone them until circumstances intervene. If we wait too long to have children, nature might make that impossible. If we don't decide to retire, our employer might make that decision for us. Even if we do eventually choose for ourselves, we often miss opportunities by taking too long, and the process leaves us miserable.

Interestingly, the situation is often not much different when we make much more trivial decisions. Where should we go on vacation? What should we make for dinner? Should we invite friends over for dinner? What movie shall we see tonight? While these decisions are insignificant beyond the moment, we once again procrastinate, fret, and regret our choices. We get upset with ourselves, and if making the decision with someone else, resent them as well. While the tension in making these decisions is high, the reward is low.

We make some choices without even realizing that we've made them. By taking too long in getting ready to go out, we miss the best movies and end up with a more limited selection. By choosing one school over another, we eliminate some possible fields of study. By letting our anxiety stop us from socializing, we don't meet the life partner of our dreams. By staying at the job we dislike, we never explore more satisfying career options. We are always choosing, even if we don't.

There is a balance between opportunity and risk, since uncertainty is scary but avoiding it might reduce our gains. When faced with a tough decision, we should first try to understand what are we afraid might happen, or what are we telling ourselves? It might also help us to take ourselves out of the equation and imagine that we were helping someone else make the decision. Stepping back to gain perspective and setting deadlines for ourselves can also reduce our anxiety and help us move on. In the end, things will happen whether we decide them or not, so we might as well choose

Chapter 6

Not All Bad

July 10

> *If we can notice a flower growing in a pile of rubbish, a ray of sunlight from an overcast sky, the laughter of a child in a crowded train station, fortune will always smile upon us.*

Aside from the crazy weather, from record heat one day to thirty degrees colder the next, crushing droughts and torrential rains, this almost seems like a normal summer. We are gathering again, going back to work, eating at restaurants, and driving everywhere. Our pandemic habits are receding – so much for take-out only, Zoom calls, and binge-watching TV. We're back, and for many of us, this is a time of relief and rejoicing. No more masks! No more social distancing! We're moving on, and the pandemic is in our rear-view mirror.

It feels almost normal, but only almost. There is pain and loss. As we continue our journey, some are missing, and many are mourning their loved ones. Others are still unwell, and many still bear the scars of loneliness and isolation. While some have decided that the pandemic is over, others still feel anxious about the most recent variant, booster vaccinations, and wondering if this will truly be over soon. Few of us will miss this pandemic, and when it's finally behind us for real, we'll be more than happy to move on.

But looking back upon these months, alongside the pain and devastation, there were also special moments and magical experiences that we risk overlooking and forgetting in our rush to reclaim our lives. First, there was the quiet. The absence of cars and pedestrians created a new space for bird song. Without the roar of airplanes overhead, it was possible to hear the rustle of the leaves in the wind. The silence, eerie at first, became delightful over time, as nature reminded us that no matter what we do to ourselves, it's still there in the background, ready to embrace us. I already miss the quiet.

The shutdown of travel and intermittent lockdowns were rough! We were torn apart from our distant friends and family members and locked in with the ones nearby. But there was also closeness in the intensity of being together all the time, as we had the opportunity to get to know each other in ways that we missed during our normal, frenzied lives. We learned how to Zoom across the country and the world, connecting more frequently with distant loved ones and reconnecting with long-lost friends. We got to know our neighbors and had family meals, cooked together, and played games. Already things feel busier, and I fear losing some of those moments.

When our favorite restaurants shut down and the movie theaters closed, we had to find alternatives. We could no longer go to museums and concerts, visit friends and travel. Stuck at home, we learned how to bake and garden. We acquired new pets and discovered painting, writing, and music. In losing most everything, we found ourselves, discovered the people around us, and reconnected with nature. Hopefully, those new activities will endure.

Chapter 7

Angry Earth

July 21

> *Thanks to our ancestors, the wooly mammoth is long extinct, but as the glaciers that hid its fate melt and disappear, the ghosts of these furry giants might rise to look askance at what we are now doing to ourselves.*

Maybe I'm paranoid, but it seems like the Earth is angry with us. Germany and China are under water, Canada is an oven, Oregon is on fire, and there's a pandemic all over the world. Everywhere you look, the Earth seems to be really upset with us. From cyclones to earthquakes, volcanos and mudslides, droughts and locusts, nature seems to be giving us hint after hint that we've overstayed our welcome. And yet, like oblivious guests that don't pick up on social cues, we stick around, taking up space and making ourselves comfortable.

Some people talk about climate change in terms of saving the Earth, but the Earth doesn't need saving. It's been around for a long time and has taken forms so hostile to life that even Mars or the upper atmosphere of Venus start looking attractive. During the Hadean epoch, which lasted 700 million years, the Earth was a glowing fireball bombarded by comets and meteors. Not the right environment for us, but Earth seemed happy enough. During the snowball Earth period (or slushball, if you prefer), the entire planet was covered with ice twice over and raked by frosty winds for millions of years. Again, not so fun for us, but no worries for the Earth. There were numerous eras in the history of the planet that would have been inhospitable for life, and especially complex life like us, but the Earth kept on spinning.

Our lives are short and our perspectives even shorter. We think in terms of days, weeks, months, and years, while to the Earth, millennia are but fleeting moments. We are also, as a species, concerned primarily with meeting our short-term interests and aren't very careful in calculating the longer-term consequences of our decisions. While we may not threaten the Earth in any meaningful way, the actions we take can certainly hasten the day when it will no longer be a comfortable home for us. After all, we are pretty fragile and can only survive within a fairly narrow band of conditions. We don't do well under water, but we can't live without it. Too hot, and we can't grow our food, and too cold, we can't plant crops in the frozen land.

While we've been warned for a while that our actions are going to make the lives of future generations more challenging, the timelineis too long for many of us to take notice. But nature isn't waiting for us to get it, and the signs of danger are all around us. As more and more places on the planet become hostile to us, we already count the cost of our decisions in human lives and economic ruin. We try to move to new locations, but soon, we will run out of those as well. We're not threatening the Earth, but we do seem to be getting on its nerves, and maybe we should start paying more attention.

Chapter 8

Summer Infestations

July 28

> *Life happens in moments. If we manage our decisions in the moment, we manage our lives.*

Every summer, our neighborhood is overrun in a new way. Some years it's been ants, crawling into our houses through every crack and crevice, threading long trails through our kitchens in search of crumbs. Other years it's been feral cats, taking over our yards like prides of lions on the savannah. For the last couple of years, it's been bunnies, rabbits everywhere, scampering across lawns and gardens, looking for fresh green stalks to eat and gardens to invade.

This year, alongside the bunnies, there is a new infestation throughout our neighborhood – dog walkers. We see them several times a day, strolling down the sidewalk with two to five dogs leashed together. Where did they come from? Why are there more multi-dog dog walkers this summer than before? Is it the gig economy? Perhaps it's the aftermath of the pandemic, when cooped up in our homes we got dogs to keep us company. Now, when the restrictions have been lifted, we are going back to work and starting to travel, but the dogs still need to go out.

So, in come the dog walkers, trailing small packs of dogs

who go about their business, sniffing bushes and hydrants and jostling among themselves. This is not criticism, mind you! I'm happy for the dog owners who enjoy their pets, happy for the dog walkers who can make a living, and happy for the dogs that get to walk and play with their friends. At the same time, the proliferation of dog walkers reminds us that the decisions we make under one set of circumstances can impact life even once those circumstances change.

We sometimes make decisions under the influence of abnormal conditions and then struggle to reconcile ourselves to the consequences of those decisions when things have gone back to normal. After being stuck at home for a year, we might decide to quit our job, sell our belongings, and hitchhike around the country, only to find ourselves alone, broke, and far away from everything we know and love once the novelty has worn away.

We are often more emotional and needy than rational in our decision-making. We get excited by some product we see advertised on TV and then buy it, only to question why we bought it when it arrives by mail a few days later. We lose perspective and get caught up in the moment, favoring immediate gratification over long-term benefit. We try to watch our diet but end up eating a tub of ice cream in a fit of sadness or distress.

Our days are made up of moments that together, like dots of color in an impressionist painting, form the big canvas of our lives. And, like those dots, each moment, each decision, leaves an imprint that indelibly alters the picture. If we slow down a bit and give time for our rational minds to catch up to our impulses, we might make fewer decisions we regret. Or instead, we can hire a dog walker.

Chapter 9

Ordinary Extraordinary

August 1

> *Once in a while, we need to take a day off, or a night, or a moment, to just give our minds a rest from the race and just be. Maybe this is the moment.*

Just an ordinary Saturday afternoon, floating down the Charles River in a kayak, enjoying the perfect weather. We reached the end point of our planned route, and somehow, it didn't feel like enough, so we went a little further, despite the prospect of having to paddle upstream on the return. Ten minutes later, we hit the jackpot, a magical spot where the trees arch over the river from both banks, forming a canopy of green that transported us from the ordinary into the extraordinary.

We lingered under the trees, soaking in the majesty and beauty, feeling like the luckiest people on the planet. Time seemed to stand still as we let the scene seep into our senses, from the dragonflies buzzing around our boats, to the breeze rippling through the leaves, and the sunlight filtering through the branches to the water. All things end, and we eventually went on our way, but the few minutes we spent in that magical corner of the river are forever etched upon the canvas of our soul.

Our lives are a continuum of moments, and we need to

cherish the good ones, because difficult times will challenge us as well. We make decisions, and those choices drive our experiences. We made the choice to kayak, despite having many other things we needed to do. We made the choice to go to this area of the river, even though it wasn't the most convenient to get to. We made the choice to go on, despite having reached the end point of our route. Our choices aren't deterministic, in that we don't control what happens, but they do influence the odds.

Luck must also smile upon us. The weather was perfect, not too hot, not too cloudy. A cool breeze made the sunshine more pleasant, and it didn't rain, as it does sometimes without much warning. We kayaked without seeing a soul, just us and the current in an intimate embrace, and floated into our emerald oasis at the perfect time of day, as the sun's rays hit the treetops at the perfect angle. Beyond this, we were lucky to have kayaks and time to use them.

Finally, while good decisions and luck are necessary ingredients for happiness, we must also keep our eyes and minds open to see the wonder when it stumbles into our path. To some, this might have just been a clump of trees obscuring the light, while others may not have noticed it at all. To experience the extraordinary, we have to look beyond the ordinary and recognize that even the mundane has the potential to be magical. Saturday, on the Charles River, it was hard not to be overwhelmed by the masterpiece of nature surrounding our kayaks, but there is wonder all around us every day if we only pay attention and seek it out.

Chapter 10

Worlds Gone By

August 7

> *We appear on this Earth and are gone in the blink of an eye. Who are we, and what will we leave behind in our wake?*

The Egyptian pharaohs sought immortality in death, constructing enormous stone structures and mummifying their bodies. Some we remember, while most were lost to the sands of time. They were not the only people throughout history to search for life beyond the grave. Many of us do. Our time on the planet is fleeting, and that is hard for us to get our minds around, so we fight the inevitable any way we can.

For some of us, the most fundamental relic we leave behind is our DNA, preserved in the lives of our descendants. Life wants to self-perpetuate, and passing our genes down to the next generation is the most basic way in which we preserve a fragment of ourselves through the centuries to come... If we are lucky. Things don't always work out that way, and even if they do, we are often still forgotten. How much do we know about our great, great, grandparents? Names? A few vague and ephemeral stories?

Some, like the pharaohs, leave physical works behind – buildings, monuments, sculptures, and other relics. Some outlast the ages, but many are worn down by sun, wind and rain, crumble into dust, or are deliberately destroyed. Even if the objects persist, over time, their connection to us gets lost. Driving into Logan airport in Boston, there is statue of Edward Lawrence Logan tucked in by the highway. While the name Logan has been preserved in the airport, few of us know of the man behind the name, and even if we look him up, we see the highlights, not the person.

We also try to find immortality by preserving our ideas thorough the stories we pass along, the writings and images we inscribe in persistent media, and the lessons we convey as parents and teachers. If not our bodies or our physical works, then perhaps our thoughts can ripple into the future, passing along our neuronal connections to others. But alas, those ideas fade, become distorted, or can be forgotten entirely. As Stephen Greenblatt points out in *The Swerve: How the World Became Modern*, much of what was written has been lost forever, and some of the most important ideas we have from the past were only preserved by accident.

So, immortality is likely beyond our reach, leaving us two choices – we can believe in heaven, an endless cycle of reincarnation, or some other form of afterlife, relying on faith or our imaginations to fill in the gaps of what we can observe. We can also entertain the possibility that our time here is all we've got, and that the pursuit of immortality should not come at the expense of living our best lives, however we define that. Either way, we choose our path, as we navigate our way from birth to death, staring into the void. The universe is vast, and we understand so little. In the end, all we have is our choices and each other.

Chapter 11

What Are We Made Of?

August 14

> *It's easy to be an optimist when things are going well and luck is breaking in our direction, but our true character shines if we can still be positive when everything goes wrong.*

Life throws us curveballs, and sometimes we strike out. We strive for success and try to get by, but sometimes things don't go our way. Disappointments are an unpleasant and potentially devastating part of our experience, and as we languish in the rubble of our hopes and dreams, it can be difficult to see a way forward or imagine a happy ending to the story. But despite our setbacks, the only viable choice is to keep going as best we can, to enshrine everything that happened today and yesterday into the history books, and to focus on tomorrow.

Of course, we have other choices, just not good ones. We can give up, forsake our dreams, abandon hope, and wallow in our misery. We can stop believing in ourselves, turn our backs on the world, and indulge in self-pity. We can become embittered, blame others or our own bad luck, engage in self-destructive behavior, or simply do nothing. There are times when this path can be tempting, as it is, at least initially, more accessible and easier to envision.

Alternatively, we can eschew the very concept of goals, focusing instead on being in the moment. We can remind ourselves that disappointment only happens when reality doesn't measure up to our expectations, and that happiness comes from letting go. There is value in reevaluating our goals and asking ourselves whether the problem was the target we had set for ourselves rather than what we accomplished. There is value in realizing that very little in life is truly important, and in learning how to just be present and aware. And yet, we might still yearn for something else and miss our hopes and dreams.

If we choose to, we can also pick ourselves up from the floor and soldier on, more determined than ever, tenacious and unrelenting. We can expand our perspective and put our disappointment in context. It's not the first time that things didn't go our way, and likely not the last either, but tomorrow is another day, full of opportunity and promise. Henry Ford built a successful automobile company after a string of failures. J.K. Rowling was rejected twelve times before finding a publisher for *Harry Potter and the Sorcerer's Stone*. We are made of tougher stuff than we know, and like many before us, we can overcome and prosper.

How can we draw upon those reserves of strength, hidden below layers of doubt, disappointment, and pain? We can start by recalling times when we succeeded in overcoming odds and transcended setbacks. If we did it then, we can do it again. We can pay close attention to what we say to ourselves, repeating positive affirmations rather than battering our souls with negative messages. And then, we can try to take one small step forward, some tiny action, that will dislocate us from the depths of our despair and rekindle our hope. Life can be tough, but so are we.

Chapter 12

Irrational Fears

August 26

> *If you're trying to help someone overcome their fears, don't ask them "What are you afraid of?" – that sounds judgmental, as if their fears are unfounded. Instead, ask "What are you afraid might happen?"*

We fear so many things these days, and we all perceive different dangers. We might be afraid of Covid-19, vaccines, the government, corporations, immigrants, police officers, autonomous cars, airplanes, strangers, spiders, or dogs. The list is endless, and we all, to some extent, become both authors and victims of our fears.

All fears are irrational. Fear is an emotion, and emotions, by definition, aren't rational. That doesn't mean that they aren't reasonable. There are some pretty dangerous things out there, and it makes sense to be scared of them. Sometimes our fears are reflexive, caused by loud noises, falling downstairs, a sudden pain, or a charging rhinoceros, and our emotional reactions kick in faster than we can think.

At other times, our fears are driven not by physical triggers but rather by a narrative we tell ourselves. We are not afraid of the thing itself, but instead by the story we construct around it. If we are afraid of walking home in the dark, it's not the dark that we fear. Instead, we imagine all the terrible things that might happen to us in the dark, and those stories drive our fears.

We might lose our way and get lost. We might fall and break our ankle. We might be attacked by bandits. All those things are possible, even if improbable, and now we are frightened. But it gets worse, since aside from the possible, our minds create stories about things that have never been. We might run into ghosts or evil spirits in the night. Aliens might land in a spaceship and abduct us. We might get attacked by werewolves or vampires.

Fear is a very powerful emotion, often driving us to action, or alternatively, paralyzing us in our place. In our fear, we might lash out at others or run away from the scary situation. The fears and the actions are just as powerful whether we are in physical danger or have constructed a story regarding a potential or imaginary threat. What exactly are we afraid might happen? Why? What are we telling ourselves right now? What do we actually know? Our fears are irrational, but we don't need to be.

Being fearful can save us, but it can also cause us harm. A fear of snakes reminds us to keep our distance, but a fear of witchcraft caused the death of many innocent people. We must therefore examine our fears carefully so that they protect us rather than hurt us or those around us. We might never get over our fears or make them go away, but if we learn to ask ourselves hard questions, we might feel better and make better choices.

Chapter 13

The Year of the Introvert

August 29

> *You have no flaws, only features. If you are impatient, channel your energy into intensity. If you are unable to focus on one thing, work on several things at once. If you feel anxious, write poetry or connect with others. Whoever you are and however you operate, work with yourself and don't think of yourself as lacking.*

Some people get energy from being around others and wither on the vine when left on their own for too long, while others become exhausted after spending time around other people and need alone time to recharge their batteries. In, *Quiet: The Power of Introverts in a World That Can't Stop Talking*, Susan Cain points out that our world caters primarily to extroverts, even though close to half of people are more introverted.

We elect leaders who appear to enjoy being among the people, and often, we describe extroverts in more positive terms. Our schools and offices are also built for extroverts, promoting a great deal of contact, and jostling among everyone and bestowing praise and glory on the loudest and most gregarious. The open office concept, which has become so common over the past few decades, is based on the idea that interaction between employees is better for the organization, at the expense of privacy or time to themselves.

This hasn't worked all that well for introverts. Walk into any open office, and you'll see people locked into their computer screens, headphones in their ears, trying to shut themselves off from the mass of people around them. Even so, they emerge each day from the mosh pit of other humans depleted, exhausted, desperate for some time alone in which to regain their strength. But, since many leaders are extroverts, and our infrastructure is derived from their needs, the challenges faced by introverts are often overlooked or undervalued.

Then Covid-19 happened, and the world turned on its head. Locked down in our homes, we were forced to learn a new way of working, in which we were alone much of the time and only interacted through limited channels. And immediately, a great howl went up from the extroverts – "How dare they keep us apart! How will we maintain our corporate culture? How will we get anything done? How will we get to know each other and have informal conversations?" Elsewhere, the cries were even louder. "No restaurants, movies, bars, clubs or concerts? No travel? No seeing relatives?" Oh, the misery!

And the introverts nestled into their homes, wearing comfortable clothing, with the dog by their side or the cat on their desk, a cup of home-made coffee by their keyboard, and got to work. They were able to think without the visual distraction of other people in their view. They were able to concentrate without hearing the murmur of voices every time a song ended. Their experience was not one of lockdown, but of freedom. Finally, able to work in an environment that suited their needs, they thrived and got a lot done.

As the pandemic winds down, many rejoice at the idea of going back to the office, but not the introverts. This was their year, and as we reconnect, we ought to do so in ways that consider their needs better than we have in the past.

Chapter 14

Lest We Forget

September 5

> *Once atop the mountain, it's tempting to feel like we got there all by ourselves and forget the many teammates, guides, support crew, family members, and friends who made it possible for us to get there.*

Labor Day is upon us, a time for beach outings, picnics, family get-togethers, and sales. For many, Labor Day marks the transition from summer to the new school year and acts as a brief pause before the pace of activity accelerates. But what is this holiday, and why are we celebrating? Labor Day was first celebrated in the late 1800s to acknowledge and appreciate the contributions of the American worker and the impact of the labor movement.

These days, union membership has dropped considerably from its heyday in the twentieth century, and many people are unclear what all the fuss was about. "Why do we need unions?" they ask, asserting that organized labor is not really relevant in today's world. While the merits and drawbacks of the labor movement are fair subject for debate, it's also the case that none of us engaged in this debate today lived in a pre-union world and experienced the working conditions of that time.

During the industrial revolution, people worked fourteento sixteen-hour days, six days a week for low wages and struggled to feed their families. Women were paid one third to one half of men's wages, children worked in factories under dangerous conditions, and about a quarter of children were injured on the job. There were no weekends, health benefits, or retirement savings for workers, all things which we take for granted today. But once we attained those benefits, we forgot where they came from.

We also forgot that without continued vigilance, these benefits could evaporate. As union membership has faded, so has the power of the worker, and corporations began taking things away. Many people work more than 40 hours a week. Retirement and health benefits have been cut back, leaving people to fend for themselves. Many people are barely getting by on a minimum wage that hasn't kept up with time. During the current labor shortage, one company advertised that it was hiring 14-year-olds. Welcome back to the nineteenth century!

Similarly, while there are legitimate concerns about our healthcare system, we have no experience of a time before vaccines, antibiotics, and science-based medicine. We don't remember a time when polio caused 15,000 cases of paralysis a year in the U.S. or when measles killed 2.6 million people a year worldwide. We don't remember a time when strep throat was a potentially deadly condition or when a simple cut could lead to a fatal infection. Not seeing the impact of unchecked disease around us, we forget what brought about our current state of health and start fearing the vaccines more than the illnesses they prevent.

Human memory is fickle, and it's natural for us to forget these things, but we do so at our peril. Once we lose sight of what got us here, we risk reversing the gains that were so hard to attain and might suffer needless misery as a result. Happy Labor Day!

Chapter 15

The Meaning of Life

September 15

> *Mars shines bright and brilliant to the east, while Jupiter and Saturn dominate the south, and beyond them, the stars twinkle in the vastness of the universe. I feel small and insignificant, but there's comfort there as well, as my worries and troubles seem smaller too.*

Since humans developed consciousness, we have been pondering the meaning of life. Philosophies, religions, academics, authors, and others have all tried to help us understand where we came from, why we are here, and what happens after we die. Many of us wake up every day hoping to make a difference in some way, to feel we've done something of value, and that our lives haven't been wasted. To some extent, the quest has so far been a failure. We have no common answers to these vexing questions, and the ideas that we've generated have had both positive and negative impacts on our well-being as a species.

Some of us have concluded that there is no meaning, and we should simply live our lives in the pursuit of happiness, however we define that for ourselves. Most other species seem to live this way, and there are many more of them than there are of us. Cats, for instance seem to focus on eating, sleeping, and chasing shadows. Animals in the wild occupy themselves with finding food, not becoming someone else's food, and replicating their species. But many of us can't do that. At some point in our prehistory, our species developed consciousness, and from that point on, has wrestled with these vexing dilemmas.

On the other hand, the search for meaning has had a huge impact on the way we live our lives, the choices we make, and the way we relate to each other. We developed rules to live by and standards for success that allow us to collaborate with others in large numbers. All cultures, societies, and religions have built narratives and values that help their members understand how to live productive lives, how to treat one another, and how to decide what is right and wrong. Unfortunately, the varied interpretation of values and meaning has also led to divisive behavior, often pitting us against each other, leading to conflict, violence, and war.

On a personal level, we're always facing difficult choices, and it's helpful for us to have guidelines along the way. In addition, the very act of striving for meaning helps us get up in the morning and gives us energy. Without meaning, our days start running into one another, and we might be prone to hopelessness or depression. So great is our need for meaning that we invent challenges and projects, enriching our lives and motivating us to look beyond ourselves, even if it does occasionally lead us astray.

We don't know the meaning of life, and likely never will, but like in many realms, asking the questions can be more valuable than determining an answer. So, the journey goes on, and wherever we end up, hopefully we can find fulfillment and happiness along the way.

Chapter 16

When Will It End?

September 19

> *The distinction between what we know and what we imagine is often unclear in our minds, but without understanding the difference, we confuse fact with fantasy and lose our way.*

As its name indicates, Covid-19 started in the fall of 2019, although many people started feeling its impact in the first quarter of 2020. Still, with 2022 only weeks away, this pandemic is already feeling way too long for many of us. Every time we think things will get better, something happens, and they get bad again. First, there was the initial panic and lockdowns, then the summer surge, then the winter surge, then the Delta variant, and it's starting to feel like things will never be normal again. Elsewhere, other surges, variants, and lockdowns happened at different times, and every time we start to relax, the virus reminds us that it's not over yet.

We hoped that warm weather would make the virus go away, but it didn't. Outbreaks continued throughout the warm weather as we started getting together again. We developed and deployed vaccines with amazing speed and stunning effectiveness, and they largely did the trick, except many people have yet to gain access to them, and too many people with access have refused them. Left with a large, global population in which to multiply and mutate, the virus has kept coming back, devastating the unvaccinated, taking us back to lockdowns and restrictions. We've done a lot to combat this virus, but based on the results, it seems we haven't done enough.

And yet, many of us are just tired of it. In some places, we have chosen to pretend that the pandemic has ended, or that it never took place in the first place. We have continued to live normally or have gone back to our normal routines, congregating in offices, eating in restaurants, watching movies in theaters, and getting together with our family members. We have turned our backs to facts and data, choosing instead to believe what we want to believe and putting our faith in people who confirm what we want to hear. Our collective attitude has shifted to denial, or at least to resignation.

We care deeply about our points of view on the topic, whatever they are, and seek out others who believe and behave as we do. But the virus doesn't care, and just keeps coming back. Its mechanism is a simple one – find vulnerable people who get close enough to each other, move between them, replicate, mutate, and keep looking for more people. If we don't understand this and act accordingly, the pandemic will linger, sickening and killing too many of us. We can't afford to be tired or frustrated, and pretending or wishing won't get us past this. We may not know exactly how to end the pandemic, but we do know how to prolong it, and so far, we're doing a good job of it.

Chapter 17

Everything is Temporary

September 26

> *To achieve peace of mind, we must let go of problems we can't solve right now, set aside our worries, and come back to them at another time. If they become urgent, they will let us know, but most likely, they will still be there, waiting patiently for us to try again, or maybe, once in a while, they will have solved themselves.*

The Earth has been around for over four billion years. From our perspective as humans, that's a very long time, almost forever, and yet it's still finite. There was a time, long ago, when our beautiful globe simply didn't exist yet. Similarly, projecting ahead another four billion years, and Earth will be no more, consumed by the sun as it enters its red giant phase. Long before that time, the oceans will have boiled off, the atmosphere will vanish into space, and the Earth will become a dry, barren rock, like Mars, only warmer and a different color.

Few things are more permanent in our minds than the Earth and the Sun, but even they have a limited lifespan. Some of us might find this idea sad or terrifying, while others might find it thrilling. As a species, we've only been around for a million years or so, agricultural for far less, and technological for hardly any time at all. If we don't annihilate ourselves beforehand, imagine what we might achieve by the time any of these astronomical events happen. At the end of the day, whether we find the demise of our solar system exciting or scary, the reality is that like everything else, our solar system is temporary.

Of course, there are far more immediate things that are visibly temporary, such as our own lives. We are born, we live out our days, and we die. Accepting the temporary nature of our lives is very difficult for many of us, as we wonder where we came from and what will happen after our death. It's sad to think that for each of us, even using the most optimistic estimates, our days on Earth are actually countable, and every night we go to sleep having lived out another, reducing our time even further.

But the temporary nature of everything is not all bad, either. We live in troubled times, but they won't last forever. The global pandemic that seems to be dragging on will, at some point, fade away or come to an end. The economic and social shocks that it has left in its wake will also work themselves out. The political turmoil and polarization that has been devastating many societies will eventually stabilize. It might take a while, and some of us may not live to see it, but the troubles we perceive in the world around us will look very different in a decade or two, and humanity will have moved on to new things.

Carl Sagan called astronomy "a humbling and character-building experience." Remembering that our planet is just a speck of dust floating in space, the third of eight planets around a medium-sized star perched in the periphery of a medium-sized galaxy, one of billions in the universe, might help us gain some perspective. Within this cosmic dance our part has been a small one. Today may be difficult or stressful, but tomorrow brings a universe of possibilities.

Chapter 18

Out of Control

October 2

> *If we let our fears determine how we live, our lives are diminished. Fear is normal, but letting it constrain our choices and define our experiences is sad and tragic. We must keep moving forward even, and especially, when we are frightened.*

We start air conditioning the house when the temperature gets a little warm and turn the heat on when we feel a slight chill. We prefer to eat only certain things at certain times, cooked in certain ways, and have routines around going to bed, getting up, and doing our work. We like to know what to expect and to live within predictable patterns, and we don't like change, especially when imposed on us by external factors.

To keep our world the way we like it, we limit our activities and confine ourselves to the familiar. We avoid traveling to new places, because it's too scary to be confronted with new languages, customs, and people. It's easier just to stay within our borders, where we know what to expect. We don't try new foods or engage in new experiences, since we're unsure of how things will turn out. Better to eat what we know and do what we've done before. It's tempting never to leave home, since everything outside our front door might be a potential threat to our reality.

Our urge to control things extends into realms where we inherently have no control. After letting go of the bowling ball, we tilt our body to one side, as if that might send the ball in the direction that we want. We wear lucky hats to sporting events, bring umbrellas to prevent it from raining, and believe that we can jinx a good outcome simply by mentioning it. We think very highly of ourselves! Or do we? Does this need for control really stem from our fear of being out of control, of not being able to handle surprises and changes that come our way?

Ultimately, our biggest fear might involve losing control of ourselves. We are emotional and may act in ways that embarrass or scare us. We worry about how other people will perceive us, carefully crafting an image and a narrative of ourselves to present to those around us, terrified that they will see through it and not like us anymore. So, we build walls and hide behind them, trying to control what happens to us and how we appear to others.

But the world doesn't work that way! We can't count on tomorrow being the same as today, and what served us well till now may not be relevant in the future. We have very little control over our circumstances, and negligible ability to impact events, and limited control of ourselves. In trying to control what we do and how people see us, we do less and have fewer genuine connections. Giving up control is scary, but holding onto it is a dangerous illusion. By believing that things might be okay even if we don't control everything, we open ourselves up to opportunities and enrich our lives, and that's a risk worth taking.

Chapter 19

Time is Finite

October 10

> *Too often, our days begin with long to-do lists and end with even longer to-do lists, as we are overwhelmed by meetings, tasks, and interruptions. Maybe we need to rethink what we're doing?*

We're born with no sense of time, living in the moment, focused on our immediate needs – food, comfort, sleep. Later, our interests become more complex as does our understanding of context, strategy, and time. We start planning and imagine different choices and their consequences. Most, but not all of us, internalize the idea that time is finite and learn how to allocate slices of time to different tasks. Some of us still struggle with this concept and miscalculate, trying to do more in a given time than is actually possible.

By overloading our schedules, we leave a trail of missed deadlines, unfinished to-do lists, and unaccomplished tasks. While overachieving may seem non-ideal, we are used to it and accomplish quite a bit in the process. We start the day with a list of twenty items that we hope to accomplish and get a handful of them done, moving the rest to tomorrow's list. Although we appear to fall short of our goals and have to live with the burden of carrying around our never-ending lists, we succeed in doing a great many things.

Unfortunately, this choice can elevate our stress level, make it difficult to work with others, and leave us disappointed, since we can never measure up to our aspirations. We may feel like we're always behind and might develop a negative narrative that paints us as deficient. We become more focused on the long road ahead than on the many miles behind us and can lose perspective as to our value. It's also difficult for us to coordinate with others, since we don't like to plan and when we try, often miss our deliverables.

Another choice involves learning how to manage our time, planning tasks based on realistic delivery schedules and building in buffer zones for mishaps and detours. For some people, this idea might seem natural, but for others, we simply don't know where to begin. We might start by putting together a realistic schedule, but then, as we get to work, remember other items and think of additional things to do. Within a short time, our schedule becomes a fantasy, a long list of hoped-for items.

A third approach goes back to living in the moment, working on one thing until we decide to focus on something else. While we may get less done this way, our lives can be quite fulfilling, as we are present in our current task without much worry about what we have completed or what might lie ahead. This approach can result in greater happiness and lower stress, though it may be difficult for us to implement if we can't let go of our aspirations and want to celebrate our accomplishments.

Time is finite, and the approach we take can impact our happiness, accomplishments, relationships, and well-being. Time doesn't change – only we can.

Chapter 20

Beyond Alternative Facts

October 23

> *If the emperor has no clothes, we might be too frightened to say so and incur the emperor's wrath, but in doing so, we sacrifice a bit of our soul. It takes courage and conviction to speak truth to power and potentially face punishment for it.*

We live in a time of alternative facts, when many of us have embraced the notion that reality isn't absolute but can be curated to conform to our beliefs. If we don't like something, we simply state the opposite and repeat our message loudly and often until it drowns out the facts and becomes the de-facto reality. We spread our ideas through social media, enlisting others, until many of us can't distinguish what is real anymore, and are ever-more dependent on leaders and sages to tell us what we should think.

This is not new. Throughout the ages, people have preferred to see what they wanted to see, averting their eyes from unpleasant realities. Ideas got propagated first through word of mouth, then through scrolls and finally print, spreading ever faster as technology allowed. As Mark Twain said, "a lie can travel around the world and back again while the truth is lacing up its boots," We imprisoned, tortured, and executed witches even though the evidence of their witchcraft was lacking. We persecuted scientists for challenging our belief that the Earth was at the center of the universe, and even in the face of overwhelming evidence, some of us insisted that the Earth was flat.

We excel at inventing stories and then justifying why they must be true. We cherry-pick and string together bits of data as proof, build up reasoning based on plausible sounding, but unsubstantiated theories, and when all else fails, lie about the facts and convince ourselves that our lies are the truth. We see everything through a distorted lens, ignoring facts that contradict what we believe and focusing only on perceptions that reinforce our world view. We either don't understand or don't want to accept the facts, and so we make up new ones that we like better.

While making up facts can be dangerous, our ability to invent fictions and collectively believe them has also been critical to our prosperity and survival as a species. In his book, *Sapiens*, Yuval Noah Harari postulated that this ability is what allows us to collaborate flexibly and in large numbers. Many of the ideas that bind us together, such as national identity, money, and corporations, are actually concepts invented by us from thin air but are none-the-less useful and necessary.

Beyond the practicalities, the human imagination is what gives color and energy to our lives. It has driven our creative endeavors, from fiction to architecture, art, drama, poetry, and film. Our childlike ability to dream and imagine has also spurred our scientific curiosity and inventiveness, helping us push boundaries and design novel solutions to problems. Although potentially perilous, our desire to believe in alternative facts highlights our awesome ability to imagine, invent, create, and connect with each other. Therefore, while it's important that we learn to distinguish fact from fiction, without alternative realities, our real lives would be diminished.

Chapter 21

Outrage and Empathy

October 31

> *Why is every day judgement day? What would happen if we adopted a curious rather than judgmental approach?*

Humans sometimes do terrible things, inflicting unspeakable cruelty upon each other, degrading and dehumanizing others. We've grown so accustomed to hearing about atrocities - people killed, displaced, stripped of rights and dignity, impoverished and abandoned, that we have become numb. Homeless people freeze on our streets, entire towns go up in flames or are swept away by floods, migrants die in the desert or drown in the sea, and prisoners succumb to torture inflicted by tyrannical regimes. We accept those things as inevitable and normal, and don't experience the outrage that might have propelled us into action. We have lost our sense of empathy, rationalized our inaction, and shifted our focus to happier thoughts.

Conversely, we have become quite sensitized to the many inconsiderate, insensitive, and downright stupid things that people do. We are easily offended when someone addresses us in the wrong way, condemn strangers for offensive words they uttered two decades ago, and refuse to forgive each other for hurtful acts, large or small, intentional or otherwise. When someone disagrees with our point of view, we go straight to outrage. When we find a word or action offensive, we respond with outrage. No matter what end of the political spectrum we are on, where in the world we live, or what we believe, we demonize each other and respond with outrage to the slightest transgression. Once again, we have lost our sense of empathy and forgotten that some time ago, or sometime soon, we will be the transgressors in someone else's frame of reference.

Our numbness to the atrocities of the world coupled with our increased sensitivity to everyday offenses makes it hard for us to distinguish the outrageous from the merely human. We have become indifferent and vengeful in equal measure, punishing those who have offended us with harsh judgment while turning a blind eye to the cruelties we so often inflict upon each other. Our apathy, as we justify the unfathomable, is bringing calamity upon us, just as our outrage at the slightest provocation stifles free thought, promotes unswerving conformity, and diminishes growth and learning. How then, do we set limits on behavior while also allowing for human error and creating a path for learning and reconnection?

The answer lies in empathy. While staking our own identities, we must recognize that we are not that different from each other. We can disagree, differ in our beliefs, and argue about ethics and morality without demonizing either one of us as evil or driving one another out of the pack. We can learn to tolerate and forgive each other's missteps while also working to eradicate cruelty and suffering. Without empathy, we fragment into factions defined by anger, judgment, and outrage. We justify cruel acts in the name of necessity or cancel those who offend us. We are us, and they are them. Outrage is easy and alluring, and sometimes appropriate, but decoupled from empathy, diminishes us and fails to make our world a better place.

Chapter 22

Bummer, Bumper, Bumpy

November 10

> *If we can enjoy the sound of the howling wind on a cold snowy day; if we can cherish the bonds we formed while in lockdown; if we can find something to appreciate throughout our difficult moments, then we are blessed with light and can guide ourselves and others through the darkness.*

The news crashes over us like ocean waves, and the wind changes daily! Some moments we are lost in a sea of anxiety, while at other times, we bask in the sunshine of unexpected delights. The volatility of the pandemic, the economy, the political environment, severe weather events, and societal strife have made living through this time feel like riding a roller coaster without a seatbelt, holding on for dear life, not knowing whether to be thrilled or terrified. It's been a bumpy ride!

And it's not over yet. There is little to indicate that things will smooth out anytime soon. We might long for a day when the news involves only sports and foliage, but this is not the time we have been born into. For good or bad, the news is overly interesting and exciting these days, drawing our attention even as it often frightens and pushes us away.

In *The 7 Habits of Highly Effective People*, Stephen Covey talks about the distinction between our circle of concern, those things we care about, and our circle of influence, what we have the power to change. For some of us, all the noise has been too much, and we have chosen to shrink our circle of concern to what we can control. We just can't deal with the news any longer and have disconnected, focusing on the small comings and goings of our own lives.

Others of us have become obsessive, checking different news sites many times a day, looking for confirmation that nothing horrible has happened while also craving the next sensationalist story. We have become addicts, loving and hating the news as we love and hate our lived experience. A happy story helps us relax and feel okay with the world while another calamity gives us the adrenaline rush of a late-night thriller on the television. We are exhausted and overwhelmed but can't turn away.

Our challenge is to steer a healthy course for ourselves through the storm by building our emotional resilience. Unlike ghost crabs, whose only choice involves crawling into the sand to hide, or moths drawn into the flame inevitably to be consumed by the fire, we possess the ability to be present in the face of the chaos without being overtaken by it.

To manage our reactions, we must first become aware of them. We need to identify that we are either overwhelmed by or drawn to the news and then to step back, breathe, and consider our choices. It might help us to write down our thoughts or talk with friends. We can try to slow ourselves down, look back into the past or think far into the future, and gain some perspective. Yes, the current situation is challenging, but the world has suffered great challenges before, and we are still here. Someday, we will go back to reading about sports and the foliage.

Chapter 23

No Plans or Goals

November 14

> *To succeed, we need to decide not only what to do, but also what not to do. Some tasks are best simplified, delegated, or eliminated entirely.*

I took a day off – no plans or goals, and it felt weird. Of course, my day was far from empty. I participated in a study group, spent time with my dad, drove someone to the airport, walked my friend's dog, ran errands for my wife, drove my son to a friend's house, went kayaking, worked on my book, took a nap, and wrote an article. But there was no goal in mind. Unusually, there was no to-do list, no schedule, and no sense of success or failure in the end. In addition, while I was pretty busy all day, there was very little structure. I did whatever came to mind, helped others where possible, and took advantage of opportunities when they presented themselves.

In all, it was a satisfying day, and one of the things that made it so was that there was no standard to measure it against. It just flowed, and whatever happened, happened. I suspended judgment, not just for later, but in concept, for the day, deciding to shed my habit of setting impossible goals, only to be disappointed in the end when I don't meet them. At the same time, it was a strange feeling, not writing tasks to accomplish on a list and not marking them off as done when I completed them. Looking back, I got a lot done, but without the pressure that I'm used to putting on myself, and it made me question my normal paradigm.

Our work and life habits get built over time, starting when we are young, and eventually become ingrained. We do things certain ways because that's what we've learned and what works for us, and we lose sight of the fact that there are many other ways to go through life and get things done that are just as productive and satisfying. Stuck in our ways, we succeed more or less, depending on the day and the tasks before us, and we are happy or disappointed based on our expectations and our achievements. But whoever we are, and whatever way we do things, our way is just one of many possible ways to live, and may not be particularly healthy or enjoyable.

To rise above the rut we may be in, we can pause once in a while, break our routines, and go about our day in a completely different manner. If our day is normally very structured, we can go with the flow. If it's chaotic, we can introduce some structure. If we generally focus just on one task, we can break it up and engage in multiple activities. If we rush around, we can slow down. By doing things in a different way occasionally, we give ourselves the opportunity to examine what we are doing and open our minds to new possibilities. In the end, we might go back to our original ways, but now with purpose rather than out of habit.

Chapter 24

Comfort in the Mundane

November 21

> *Some see weeding the garden as drudgery, while others see it as fun. Some find it boring, while others meditative. Some hate getting dirty, while others love the connection to the soil. Choose to see the positive and make the most of any situation.*

My day-to-day is hectic and busy, ruled by schedules and lists, often presenting me with difficult problems to solve and challenges to overcome. Every day it feels like there are dragons to slay and mountains to climb, as well as an overwhelming list of smaller tasks to accomplish. Some days, I wake up already behind, slightly breathless and overwhelmed. Other days, I set forth full of energy, delving deep into the pile until weariness overtakes me or I run into a riddle I can't solve. Sometimes I don't get stuck, but one task takes me five times longer than expected, knocking everything else off track.

I'm not special in having such a schedule or in trying to do too much. Many of us take on more than we can really do, and it can be quite overwhelming. We might exhaust ourselves trying, or give up part-way, or start plodding along like zombies in the night, unfeeling and only half alive. Alternatively, we could plot a different course, being more selective in what we decide to undertake and learning to say "no" when asked by others to overburden ourselves. While it's a great practice to set limits on ourselves and boundaries for others, there are also costs involved in choosing to do less, and some of the tasks on our plate are beyond our control to refuse.

Despite this, whatever we decide to do, and whatever lies waiting on our plate, we still control our attitude and can shape our experience of events. If we can accept the inevitable without bitterness or anger and learn to be aware of our choices as we make them, we can make the best of our circumstances. We need to let go of what we don't control, but also to make thoughtful decisions where we have some leeway. We can choose to emphasize the positive, and even if circumstances are dire, to look for little bright spots within the gloom.

There is comfort in the mundane. I woke up this morning and cleaned the kitchen, approaching it not as a chore but as a comforting routine. First the dish rack, then the bottom rack of the dishwasher, then the silverware, and finally the glasses in the top rack. The process was slow, routine, mundane, the familiar clatter of dish upon dish reassuring in my ears. As I finished loading a new batch of dirty dishes into the dishwasher and wiped down the counters, the kettle boiled, heralding the brewing of some English breakfast tea and the start of the new day. There is joy in the routine and comfort in the familiar.

I looked around at the clean kitchen, pleased with a job well done, and took my mug of tea to the other room and the challenges that awaited me. If we appreciate the little things, life is more pleasant, the mountains are less daunting, and the dragons are less frightening. Long live the mundane!

Chapter 25

Learning Greek

November 28

> *When we read the news, do we want to explore new or different perspectives or are we simply looking to confirm what we already believe?*

Many years ago, in college, I had to learn the Greek alphabet. At the time, it seemed like a fun, but not too practical, intellectual exercise. Now, it's coming back to me, and feels less fun, and much more practical. Just this week, some parts of the world have been shutting down again due to the Omicron variant of the Covid-19 virus while other areas are still struggling with the lingering effects of the Delta variant. And who can forget the Alpha and Beta variants that popped up last year or the Gamma variant that devastated Brazil.

But if pandemics aren't your thing, let's talk about the weather. In 2020, the Atlantic hurricane season tallied thirty storms, running out of names and using Greek letters to fill in the rest. Alpha, Beta, Gamma, Delta, Epsilon, Zeta, Eta, Theta, and Iota all made it into our vocabulary, with Alpha, Zeta, Eta, and Iota all making landfall, causing over 400 deaths and over $50 billion worth of damage. Who knew that the Greek alphabet would come in so handy again!

Greek philosophers and scientists were central to the development of modern, Western civilization. They pioneered rational thought, mathematical proofs, geometry, basic science, and other disciplines, emphasizing logic and the rational, impartial observation of the natural world. While their understanding was limited by technology and their thinking was constrained by the social norms of their day, they laid the foundation for much of what we have today. Modern medicine, scientific breakthroughs, and technological feats such as the cell phone or airplane would not be possible without the ideas broached by the early Greek thinkers.

It's even more distressing, then, that we seem to be moving away from rational thought while ever-more dependent on it. Why is belief in climate change more dependent on one's political affiliation than on the underlying science? Why are people's attitudes towards vaccines based more on the news sources or social media groups they connect to rather than on the statistical probability of getting sick, dying, or propagating the virus? It has become nearly impossible for many people to distinguish between scientific fact and fictional hysteria, as intentional misinformation and fake news spread using technology that wouldn't exist without the very scientific thinking they reject.

But the natural world doesn't care what we believe or what news sources we follow. Violent storms wash over us, and wildfires destroy entire communities, whether the inhabitants recognize or deny global warming. Our hospitals are full, and millions have gotten sick and died despite the fact that some of us don't believe the virus threat is real. Instead of relearning the Greek alphabet, let us therefore face these challenges by embracing the rational, scientific thinking of the ancient Greeks.

Chapter 26

Angry

December 6

> *According to Mark Twain, "Anger is an acid that can do more harm to the vessel in which it is stored than to anything on which it is poured." In order to release ourselves from the prison of our minds, we need to have actual conversations with real people.*

It seems like everyone is angry these days. Some are angry at immigrants for coming into the country, while others are angry at those who stop immigrants from entering the country. We are upset with the police, frustrated with protestors, and furious at politicians. We are angry with doctors who take care of us, teachers who educate our children, drivers, cyclists, pedestrians, neighbors, and most anyone else. We march, shake our fists, go to court, and in the extreme, get violent. Anger spills from screens into our homes, spreading anxiety and fueling more anger in its wake.

Anger isn't a stand-alone emotion but, instead, reflects helplessness and fear. If we feel confident and secure, we don't need to be angry. Whatever happens, we can deal with it. Whatever others say or do, we let go and take in stride. Feeling strong, we have empathy for others and reach our hands out to help them. Perhaps our pervasive anger is a symptom of our stress and helplessness, and the fear that things can only get worse than they are right now.

The Optimistic Pessimist

We've had financial stress and economic uncertainty. Whole industries have disappeared or shifted elsewhere, as globalization and market forces changed the landscape. When we are afraid for our jobs, we view other nations as competitors and immigrants as threats. The pandemic has also made us wary of each other, not sure who to trust or what information to follow. We are literally scared for our lives, and the information out there is bewildering. No wonder we're angry. Climate change seems beyond our ability to manage, and the threat of nuclear war grows daily, highlighting our loss of control. We want a better world but can't imagine how to get there.

Social media hasn't helped, of course. Too many of us are locked into echo chambers, communicating only with people who share our beliefs and amplify our fears. Rampant and intentional misinformation by politicians, influencers, and others only makes us even more fearful, frustrated, and hateful. We long for the mythical happy days of old and gravitate toward authoritarian leaders who exploit our fear and anger to gain power and control.

There is another choice! We can regain our optimism, embrace hope and opportunity, and look to the future with excitement rather than fear. As a species, we didn't take over the planet by being fearful and angry, but instead by being curious, resourceful, and inventive. We collaborated with each other to overcome challenges, experimented, explored, and pursued impossible dreams, turning them into reality. Instead of clinging fearfully to what we've got, angry that "they" might take it away from us, we can regain our confidence, smile in the face of adversity, and work together to reclaim the bounty of our world.

Chapter 27

The Small Stuff

December 16

> *My grandmother used to say that "very few things in life are truly important, so we should focus on the few important ones and let go of the rest." If we allow ourselves to get stressed over trivial matters, we exhaust ourselves and diminish the quality of our lives. So before getting hot and bothered, we should ask ourselves if this is one of those few important things. Much of the time, it won't be, and we can relax and be happier.*

In 1997, Richard Carlson published his best-selling book, *Don't Sweat the Small Stuff ... and It's All Small Stuff*. This book, one of his many influential writings, hammered home the idea that we control our thoughts, and that we can choose what to do and where to focus. It reminded us that most of the things that upset us aren't important enough to get worked up over, and that even if they are upsetting, letting ourselves get upset by them isn't going to help us.

It's so easy to find everything upsetting. For many months, our lives have been dominated by a pandemic that scared us and restricted our choices. Every time we imagine life going back to normal, there's another setback, and we don't know what we're supposed to do and what advice to follow. The whole thing feels like a cruel guessing game, and we yearn so much for our old lives. How could we not be upset?

Beyond the pandemic, there are many other things that can

make us unhappy. Let's talk politics, or maybe not, because we can't even say the word without upsetting someone or ourselves. How about the economy... Inflation anyone? Income inequality? Perhaps culture and society... can you say discrimination, cancel culture, racism, the big lie, the big steal, transgender rights, abortion.... It feels like there's no place to turn without getting upset.

We can't enjoy a sixty-degree day in December without remembering the climate catastrophe it heralds. Planting tomatoes in the garden, we think of the contaminants that might be in the soil or seeping into our drinking water. Tornados and fires tear through our towns while our coastal cities are increasingly underwater. Even our loved ones are annoying, now that we've spent too much time together through lockdowns, and our favorite TV shows keep getting pushed off the air.

We are sweating everything, and our frustration is at a boiling point. We look for answers, demonize each other, see conspiracies everywhere, and act out in horrible ways. Not only are we upset, but we have allowed our anger and frustration to define us. And it only seems to be getting worse.

This is the perfect time to remember that we shouldn't sweat the small stuff, and that everything is small stuff. Humanity has survived more devastating pandemics, worse economic times, scarier political environments, and more horrible cultural and social rifts. Without minimizing the difficulty many are going through, it's still helpful to take some perspective. More importantly, while we don't control events, we still decide how to respond, and can choose to let go and be positive.

Chapter 28

De-Graded

December 18

> *Some problems don't have simple solutions, no matter how hard we try or hope they might.*

This was grading week at the university, and thankfully it's over. My grades have been submitted, and now I get to recover my sanity for a few weeks until a new semester begins. Every term, it's the same thing all over again. I construct a syllabus with a grading scheme that tries to be as fair as I can make it. That isn't an easy task, because constructing graded assignments is a nontrivial affair.

If I want the assignments to be meaningful, to constitute a learning experience in their own right, they become excruciatingly difficult to grade. Much as I try, it's hard to evaluate creative thinking, the application of ideas, or the extrapolation of theory into new realms. Not impossible, but difficult, so much so that it becomes too challenging to assign to a teaching assistant.

Alternatively, I can construct assignments and assessments that are easy to grade, but then they feel like meaningless, artificial exercises meant only to assign scores and let me move on. How meaningful is a multiple-choice test when the only way to differentiate between students is to give them nuanced, gotcha answers that can be interpreted multiple ways and ask them to read my mind. Sure, those are easy to score, but in the end, the whole exercise feels rather hollow.

And why are grades so important, anyway? When I was in business school in the 1990s, I worked hard, got great grades, and finished my MBA with high honors. In the ensuing twenty-six years, not one person has ever asked me about those grades. No one cared how I did on my corporate finance final or how the professor liked my strategy paper. The only thing they seemed to care about was that I now had the letters MBA following my name and that it came from a school they recognized.

Of course, I enjoyed the personal satisfaction of doing well, but at the end of the day, it wasn't very important. In fact, there are some studies that show that grading actually interferes with learning, as students focus on trying to play the game rather than on learning as much as they can. Assessments and assignments can be meaningful, but looking at the effort we spend on grading and how it impacts student behavior, it feels like we're on the wrong track, stuck in an archaic system that serves itself rather than enhancing curiosity, learning, knowledge, growth, and connection.

Our lives our finite, and we need to be thoughtful as to how we spend our days. Grading feels like a waste of time, whether because our assessments are meaningless or because they are so complex that they take us too much time to evaluate. There's got to be a better way! I wish I had an answer, but I really don't. Instead, what keeps me going is knowing that the grading is finite, while the higher purpose of learning and exploration will endure long after the grades have been forgotten.

Chapter 29

The Day After

December 26

> *We are about to enter a new year, and it feels like I need to say something profound but it's also important to keep things in perspective and to remember that today is Thursday and tomorrow is Friday and the world keeps revolving around its axis and around the Sun. It's just another day, and that's a good thing too.*

For many people around the world, today is the day after Christmas. For others it might be the day after their birthday. For astronomy buffs, it is the day after the launch of the James Webb space telescope. Whatever day it is for you, if it is the day after something special, it might be a wonderful time in which you could bask in the joy of what has just come to pass. Alternatively, it might be a day of disappointment if the much-anticipated day fell short in some ways. Of course, it might be neither, but instead just another ordinary day. Yesterday was Saturday, and today is Sunday, just like any other week. Yesterday was the 25th, today is the 26th, and tomorrow will be the 27th. Special days are significant to us because of the stories we attach to them, whether religious, cultural, or personal. After all, for many people in the world the 25th is just another day, while for others, it is deeply meaningful. Most people in the world probably didn't even know that the James Webb Space

Telescope lifted it off yesterday, but for those of us who care, it was the culmination of decades of work and the dawning of a new age in scientific discovery. Of course, these events have consequences independent of our narratives. For example, the space telescope employed thousands of people, cost billions of dollars, took decades to build, and might not only help us understand how the universe formed, but also help us find life on other planets.

But all that happened yesterday, and today is the day after. Turning the page can be difficult, whether the previous chapter was wonderful or problematic. We are starting over, and that requires energy that we might not have, feeling depleted after reaching the milestone or celebrating the day. The rush to the pinnacle gave us a rush of adrenaline, which then started draining away as we stood at the peak and admired out surroundings. On the day after, we might feel lost, not knowing where to go next or what to do with ourselves. We were so focused on the day, that now, we've lost our compass, for a moment, and don't know which way to turn.

But we don't have to go anywhere for now. We can learn to relax and just enjoy the day, perhaps even feel relieved that for an instant, we aren't on a quest. The day after the holiday, we can rest, clean up, tell stories, and be present with ourselves. Sometime in our future, there will be another goal, another day to anticipate and plan for, another achievement to work toward. The journey will continue, and we will put one foot in front of the other once again, but not today. Today is the day after, and that's a good thing. Life is a series of moments, and whether we are anticipating, celebrating, or resting, we are okay. Enjoy this day!

Chapter 30

Done with Covid

January 2

> *I wish I were wiser, taller, younger, more handsome than I am, but wishing for things doesn't make them true.*

Twice recently, people told me that they are "Done with Covid." I didn't realize we had that option. Had I known, I would have been "Done with Covid" two years ago before it started. While I understand the sentiment behind such statements, I also question them. This has been one stubborn, unpredictable virus. Some of us believed the whole thing was overblown, while others of us were nervous that it would kill us all. Either way, some people got sick while others were untouched, some were hospitalized or died, while others had mild cold symptoms. The virus didn't tell us what it was going to do and didn't care what we believed.

Some say that this latest variant is so contagious that we will all get infected at some point, so why be cautious. This is a fatalistic approach that can lead to reckless behavior. We can still take measures to protect ourselves, and the longer we delay getting infected, the better doctors can learn how to treat the disease. By taking precautions, we can also make it more likely that even if we do get sick, it won't be as badly. We are playing a game of odds, and we should try to give ourselves the best chance to obtain a good outcome.

Others are saying that they want to get infected in order to develop immunity. We can't afford to be this arrogant when it comes to Covid-19. Even though the most recent variant seems to be less lethal than the ones that came before it, especially for people who are fully vaccinated, there are still people getting sick and dying from the disease. Lower odds don't mean smooth sailing for all, and some of us who want to get the virus will get more than we bargained for. In addition, it's not clear how long our immunity will last, or how we might fare against the next variant that comes along.

Finally, with more people getting diagnosed, the virus has a bigger community of hosts in which to mutate and form new variants. Generally, viruses become more virulent but less deadly over time, but that's the long-term trend. Over the short term, some of the variants that develop might surprise us in very unpleasant ways, and this has been a particularly enigmatic virus.

Covid-19 has dominated our world for nearly two years. Fatigue has set in, and we really want it to be over. We want things to go back to normal and we need our lives back. We also know much more now than we did two years ago. We will find a way forward, but we can't afford to be fatalistic, arrogant, or complacent. Some day we will be "done with Covid," as it will either disappear or become endemic like the common cold, but to get there, we need to follow the science and make smart choices rather than simply declare our wish and hope things go our way.

Chapter 31

Nothing is Real

January 8

> *It's only early January, and I've already broken some of my New Year's resolutions. But on the bright side, there are still a few that have managed to hang on, and they might make all the difference.*

I have a love-hate relationship with the news. I find it fascinating, since over the world, and even in Space, there are so many interesting things to learn about. I also find it irritating, because much of the news isn't really news, but instead interpretation or commentary. In addition, we are as likely to get our news from social media as we are from moderated sources, so the line between fact and narrative has blurred to the point where it's very difficult to tell them apart.

Scanning news sites regarding any event, more stories analyze the event or tell us what some person said about it than describe what actually happened. Even within the story itself, fact and analysis are interwoven in the same sentences, as much by what is said as by what is omitted. This is not new but has become more pronounced as the news industry has become subjected to commercial pressures and driven by the need to provide 24-7 entertainment.

At least mainstream news outlets have professional standards and make some efforts to separate news from opinion, with more or less success. On social media, not only is there no attempt to verify facts, but people also make overt attempts to misinform. Any statement goes, and while we argue with each other using ever more forceful language, little of what gets said helps us differentiate fact from fiction. We've stopped trying to validate stories and instead base our beliefs on who has said them, putting our faith in messengers we trust, no matter how unsubstantiated or absurd their assertions.

With all that noise, it seems like nothing is real. If nothing is factual, then any belief is equally valid, and opinions matter as much as facts. But going too far down that road is dangerous, since at the end of the day, there is a reality that underlies all our narratives. We believe what we want to believe and cherry-pick news items that confirm our preconceived notions. We are a pattern-seeking and story-telling species, more emotional than rational.

Our challenge is to believe less and question more, neither accepting nor dismissing ideas but instead seeking out evidence. If we can change something by believing the opposite, then it's not factual. Reality doesn't care what we believe and will remain unchanged. We might argue over the causes of climate change but can measure parts per million of carbon dioxide in the atmosphere. We must question our sources of information and purposely seek out differing points of view, so we can sift through the opinions and examine what remains. Reality still exists, even if it's hard to see through our narratives and it might surprise and punish us for our negligence if we don't work harder to seek it out.

Chapter 32

Beyond the Red Giant

January 19

> *Today is our day, a moment in time, once and gone forever, and we must live it to the fullest.*

Sometime in the future, in four or five billion years, the Sun will run out of hydrogen and start expanding, turning red and swelling to beyond the orbit of the Earth. Long before, in fewer than one billion years, changes to the Sun's luminosity along with magnetic and tectonic changes on Earth will cause the planet to heat up and the oceans to evaporate. At that point, the Earth will become a dry, barren planet, as uninhabitable as Venus is today. An alien space probe, looking for life in solar system, might not suspect that we were ever here, as mighty forces erase all traces of our existence.

Of course, a billion years is a long time, and by then, we will have either become a spacefaring, multi-world species or driven ourselves into extinction, so there's no need for panic yet, but the end is still unsettling. We want to imagine a future, and it's painful to think that not only our species might be gone someday, but every living creature on Earth might disappear from the galactic record. Someday there might be nothing here but molten rocks and radiation, leaving no trace of life for others to recognize. We will be gone, forever and completely.

On a more personal level, we know that every living creature is on the clock, only here for a certain amount of time and doomed to die. That, too, is unsettling, for looking ahead, we like to think that there is a future for us and have a hard time getting our minds around the idea that someday we will be gone. How many generations back do we really know our ancestors, and even if we know their names, what else do we know about them?

In time, we fade from memory, and the Earth continues to spin around without us, as if we were never here. Few of us make lasting impact, and even they are limited and diminish with time. The ancient kings of Babylon, Pharaohs of Egypt, or emperors of China created dynasties that lasted hundreds of years, but where are they today? Unable to comprehend an ending, we imagine alternative scenarios in which we never completely disappear, ending up in Valhalla or heaven, reincarnated or ethereal. What really happens when we die, we don't know, but we definitely don't continue as we are.

While it's sad to think that someday we and everything around us may be gone, we are also reminded to make the most of the time we have. If we learn to appreciate and enjoy the wonders of our planet, the companionship of friends and loved ones, and the joys that imagination and adventure can provide us, our time here will not have been wasted. Yes, it's all temporary, but there is so much to do and experience. While the journey will end someday, we choose how to live our lives today and every day and can create in every moment an eternity.

Chapter 33

Hot and Cold

January 23

> *Setbacks and challenges happen, but we must keep moving forward undaunted, taking each day as it comes, focusing on the small wins and the big picture. It may be dark out now, but Venus is rising, and dawn will come.*

Today, the heat went out in part of our house. I woke up shivering and discovered that during the night, the temperature outside had dipped to -11 C, and some pipes had frozen, preventing hot water from circulating in the radiators. Of course, this happened on a weekend! Fortunately, our heating system consists of multiple zones, and some of them were still working, so I cranked up the heat and waited. By noon, one area started warming up, but the other stayed stubbornly chilly, as the frozen pipe had not yet thawed. Eight hours later, the final zone started working again, and I breathed a sigh of relief.

Fortunately, no harm was done, and the cost was largely non-financial – some stress and wasted time. None of that is important or particularly interesting. What is significant was the degree to which this incident impacted my entire day and the ways I tried to manage myself through it. I can't deny that I was stressed, mostly because of the timing; it's nearly impossible to find a plumber who can come quickly this time of year. How stressed? I couldn't concentrate on work and I found myself less patient in my interactions with my family. I just wasn't at my best, and while I knew it and tried to protect others from adverse impacts, I was not entirely successful.

The day seemed eerily normal, considering how I felt. I did the things I typically do on a Saturday and even connected with some family and friends, but hanging over it all was this worry, and my insides felt different than my outside appeared. While I'm pleased with how things turned out (no plumber, no flood, and, eventually, heat), and generally fine with the actions I took to get there, I'm less happy with the way I managed my emotions.

Life throws curve balls at us, and our challenge is to manage them on both the tangible and emotional levels. For me, focusing on solving the problem helped, while waiting to see if the solution worked was difficult. The longer I waited, the more I spun out worst-case scenarios and contingency plans. Managing my fears of what might be, especially given the uncertainty, was hard, though talking about it with others helped a bit. I had to negotiate with my negative narratives and try to be optimistic that my solutions would work.

I often counsel people to manage their emotions and stay positive, and while I was mostly successful in doing so, I was reminded that none of this is easy when a situation presses our buttons, and we are emotionally compromised. Advice, even good advice, is much easier to give than to follow.

Chapter 34

The Blizzard of 2022

January 29

> *We can't see over the horizon or around the bend, but that doesn't mean that the world is flat or is limited to our field of view.*

This weekend, we experienced one of the most serious blizzards in recent memory. With snow accumulations of thirty inches in some places, and winds hitting ninety miles an hour, the last weekend in January seemed appropriately wintery. Couple this storm with temperatures plunging into negative territory overnight, and it becomes easy to imagine that climate change isn't happening. This is the kind of wintery weather we experienced in New England five decades ago, so clearly nothing has changed.

Only it has! Despite the recent cold spell and the weekend blizzard, the average temperature has been rising every decade, glaciers are melting in the poles and on the mountains, and severe weather events, including this blizzard, are more likely. There is a difference between climate and weather, and while our particular location might experience a cold winter, on a global scale, the amount of carbon dioxide in the atmosphere is increasing, and the planet is warming up.

Why is it that we struggle to see the big picture? In their book, *Thinking Fast and Slow*, Kahneman and Tversky called this phenomenon WYSIATI (What You See Is All there Is). Our minds collect local information that we experience directly and construct a narrative of reality based on our observations. If we experience a blizzard or our local temperatures drop below freezing, it is therefore natural for us to imagine that the whole world is cold and to have a hard time accepting that despite our local weather, it's actually warmer overall.

Even when confronted with ample evidence of a hotter Earth, we have a hard time unraveling our story. Wildfires, droughts, floods, hurricanes, tornados, and other disasters impact more people throughout the world, and yet we fail to see the connection to climate change, instead regarding each instance as an isolated, local phenomenon or an act of God. Climate scientists predicted these patterns and warned us decades ago, but even now, faced with previously predicted consequences, we fail to connect the dots.

While our brains are optimized for pattern recognition, climate change is hardly the only area where we miss the forest for the trees. If we don't personally know someone who has been hospitalized due to Covid, then we don't imagine it to be a serious threat to our health. If we hear of someone winning millions in the lottery, we forget that governments use lotteries to raise funds, and that a vast majority of people lose their money.

Given our predisposition to make poor assessments using only local information, we need to recognize that we are prone to making bad decisions based on distorted narratives of reality. We therefore need to become skeptics, in the healthy sense of the word, and to demand hard evidence before we draw conclusions. We need to ask ourselves and others tough questions and to respond to events like scientists rather than storytellers. The stakes are high, and we need to see beyond the blizzard.

Chapter 35

Moving On

February 5

> *Progress is seldom linear, and setbacks don't necessitate failure. If we step back, look at a longer time horizon, and approach our goals with a sense of perspective, the daily ups and downs don't feel as significant.*

We make decisions every day, many times a day. Sometimes, we choose well, but often make decisions we regret or come to see as non-ideal. Similarly, despite our best efforts to be careful, we make mistakes all the time, at times costly ones, damaging our own interests and possibly hurting others along the way. Looking back, it's easy to second-guess ourselves and judge our decisions harshly, forgetting that we didn't know then what we know now and merely did our best with the information we had.

Or did we? How often are we really at our best? Too often we are distracted or tired, self-absorbed or narrow-minded. We act on impulse and rationalize bad behavior, even when we know the likely consequences. At our core, we are emotional creatures ruled by irrational concerns and chemical reactions in our brains, often at odds with our strategic objectives. We are at times cruel or harsh, self-centered or inattentive, and scared or self-protective. Later, after the impulse passes, and the dust settles, it's easy to view our decisions with derision.

Sometimes we view with judgment not only the things we have done, but also what was in our minds. We may have wished for bad things to happen to someone else or jumped to conclusions about people and situations. We may have devalued another person or dismissed someone from our minds. We may have allowed our minds to wander when we needed to focus or got distracted when someone was desperate to be heard. We are all so very flawed as we try to muddle through.

Forgiveness is difficult, when it comes to letting go of the hurt imposed upon us by others but forgiving ourselves can be even harder. We might remember every poor decision, errant thought, and unfortunate interaction where we didn't make ourselves proud and wish we had done things differently. It's easy to get stuck in the past, looking at our spotty track record with hateful sorrow. Strangely, there can be some comfort in beating ourselves up for things we can no longer change.

But time only moves forward. Whatever happened, whatever we did, is now beyond our reach, and we are once again faced with new choices, including how we deal with what happened in the past. Some of us might try to forget, leaving things out of our story or rewriting it entirely. This is a dangerous choice, for in it we learn nothing, setting ourselves up for more regrettable decisions. Others of us might get caught in a loop, reliving our past failures, and losing connection with the present in all of its wonder and opportunity.

The challenge is therefore to learn from our past, including our indiscretions and unfortunate decisions, to acknowledge and address what we can, and then forgive ourselves and let go of what can no longer be changed.

Chapter 36

The Great Reset

February 16

> Ah, the good old days – how we miss them! But do we really? Do we really want to go back to flip phones, rotary-dial phones, the telegraph, or papyrus? Nostalgia can be dangerous if left unchecked.

There is excitement in the air as the Omicron variant fades, and it feels like we are finally putting the pandemic behind us. We miss our lives before the pandemic. We miss traveling and seeing people, going out to restaurants and bars, attending concerts and theater, seeing movies, and even going to the office. We've felt so lonely and isolated and miss human company so much that we've started to wax nostalgic about going to work.

Really?

Prior to the pandemic, how much of our time did we spend complaining about our jobs? Did we really love commuting in traffic, getting agitated and worrying about road-rage? Parking was so much fun, whether we had to find space in an over-priced and cramped garage or hunt for elusive spots on the street. Did we enjoy riding the subway, crammed so close to other commuters that we could hear the music from their headphones?

Do we really miss sitting in meetings, staring at slide decks, hearing people drone on about their weekly status and trying to stay awake enough that no one notices we've checked out? Are we longing for office politics and having people judge what we're wearing, when we arrive and leave, and what we eat for lunch? Have we really been away from work for so long that we've forgotten how much of office life was annoying and oppressive? I think we have, but I don't think it will take us too long to remember once the day-to-day grind of office life resumes.

Having company as we work is, overall, good for us, but as we contemplate returning to the office, we also have an opportunity to examine how things were before and make some improvements. We can use the disruption of the pandemic as a reset, restructuring our entire concept of work to optimize interaction while incorporating elements of flexibility, individualism, and work-life balance from the past two years.

How can we travel smarter to work? What is the best use of our time when we're together, and what works better if we're home? How can we integrate our work and family lives more happily? Everything that happens can be a lesson for the future, including the pandemic. Sure, we can go back to our old office life if we want to, but unless we focus forward and create a better work environment, our excitement will be short-lived.

Chapter 37

Invisible Anxiety

February 20

> *Feeling stuck? Bored? Anxious? Try something new today! Break your routine. Eleanor Roosevelt said, "Do one thing every day that scares you." Even one tiny step might bring a little ray of sunshine.*

Everything seems a little more difficult these days and a lot more stressful. Two years of pandemic followed by war, inflation, layoffs, political turmoil, financial uncertainty, and natural disasters have left us jittery and wary, waiting for the next calamity to descend.

We're back to traveling, but now, there's more to it than buying tickets, finding our passports, and getting on a plane. The passport office seems to be in disarray, airlines cancel flights willy-nilly and sometimes go out of business entirely, weather events disrupt our plans, strikes shut down whole countries, and everything is more expensive. Our supermarkets are out of eggs, and if we can find them, they cost twice as much as they used to. Used cars went up in price and then back down just as mortgage rates went down and then back up. We quiet quit our jobs only to get laid off, got caught in a tug of war between our dogs and our bosses over going back into the office, and stopped talking to each other for fear of offending or engaging in conflict. It's been a challenging time!

Yet, we go on! We adjusted to working remotely, and then hybrid, and back to working side by side in an office. We figured out ways of seeing people on screen and then tried to remember how to socialize in-person. We picked up hobbies and adopted pets, learned to cook and garden, and made the best of things, only to have to find dog walkers as we left our homes and started commuting to the office again. We are an adaptable species.

But all is not well. The events of the last two years have driven us into a state of anxiety, invisible to others and often to ourselves. With the prevailing uncertainty, helplessness, and fear, it's no wonder that we're feeling anxious, even as we focus on getting on with our everyday lives. We're trying to pretend that we can power through this, and that everything's okay, but it's not. The signs are everywhere.

We try to sleep but suffer from insomnia. We've learned to cook but overeat, snacking to calm our nerves. We drive less but get into more accidents. We spend more time on social media but feel more disconnected. And the macro-trends are terrifying. Violent crime is up, overdose deaths are up, mental illness is getting worse, racism parades itself openly in the town square, and we can't even talk to each other without demonization and name-calling. We are far from okay.

This pandemic is passing, and things are starting to feel more normal. But prolonged, untreated anxiety leaves scars, and unless we have a plan to address it, the personal and social toll of the last couple of years will extend well into the future. We have to learn to talk about our anxieties and develop skills and strategies to manage them, and more than anything else, we need to recognize that we are all in this together and reach out to each other with empathy and understanding.

Chapter 38

Henchmen

February 27

> *Too often we forget the solid, plodding souls that put things back together while we slumber. Too often do we take them for granted, but we do so at our peril, since we depend upon them far more than we would like to admit.*

We see them in movies – henchmen acting on behalf of evil villains. They run into the middle of our screens only to get cut down by the good guys. They pursue heroes in endless car chases, always shooting, rarely hitting, only to crash and burn around some bend. They take a lot of punishment, these henchmen, and things rarely go well for them, and yet, there seems to be an endless supply of these people.

Bad people do bad things for their own self-interest. You have a toy. They want this toy and try to take it away from you by any means necessary. If things go their way, they end up with the toy. The same is true for adults, whether we are looking at fictional movie villains or real-life dictators, criminals, or other ruthless, self-interested bullies. The person at the top, the bad actor, wants to end up with the toy, be it money, territory, or power.

But the same can't be said for their henchmen. In, *Freakonomics*, Steven Levitt and Stephen Dubner discuss why

"Drug Dealers Still Live With their Moms." Research by University of Chicago student, Sudhir Venkatesh, determined that drug runners, the henchmen of the drugs hierarchy, average only $3.30 an hour while working jobs with the highest risk for violence, extortion, and arrest. The probability that they might one day move up the gang hierarchy is tiny, and yet, they still do it, and we never run out of runners.

Criminals, politicians, generals, or business leaders often treat their henchmen as expendable extensions of their own will, disdainfully putting them in harm's way. They expect complete loyalty from their followers while offering none in return. Without Crabbe and Goyle, the Malfoys of this world are powerless, yet they abandon their henchmen willfully. Corrupt politicians retire wealthy, while their supporters go to prison. Factory owners build palaces, even as their workers sink deeper into debt.

So, who are these followers, and why are there so many of them? Sadly, we are these henchmen! We look for leadership, often in the wrong places. We mistake arrogance for strength and are attracted by charisma and vision. We develop loyalty to leaders and overlook the evil acts they push us to perform. We stop thinking for ourselves and blindly follow orders we know to be wrong. We kill, injure, exile, imprison, torture, impoverish, cheat, humiliate, and dehumanize others, repeating convenient stories to rationalize our behavior.

This is wrong! We need to treat others as we would want to be treated ourselves, and to follow an internal moral compass based on empathy and compassion. Otherwise, we've seen this movie before. The henchmen perish and are forgotten, and we don't want to be them.

Chapter 39

Cousins

March 8

> *Conflict is a normal and healthy part of life – it's fine and often productive for us to disagree with each other. How we go about resolving it? Now, that's the question, isn't it?*

We are closely related to the great apes and, in particular, to chimpanzees, with whom we share 98.8 percent of our DNA. Like chimpanzees, we are highly social, deriving our sense of belonging and security from one another and living within the norms of our societies. Chimpanzees are generally territorial, dividing into troops led by aggressive males and waging often violent war on neighboring clans with the hope of gaining foraging space and food. War parties go out into adjoining patches of forest, chasing away other troops, maiming and killing rival chimpanzees, including youngsters, who can't escape quickly enough.

Chimpanzee societies are hierarchical, ruled by the largest, most powerful, overtly aggressive males. These dominant males govern by force, overpowering other males in their group and forcing themselves onto females within their domain. Females and lesser males who conform to their leaders' will lead quiet, peaceful lives, while any dissent is suppressed violently and swiftly. Once the hierarchy is established, chimpanzee society is generally benign most of the time, with strong communal bonding and supportive behavior within the clan; this situation can remain stable for long periods, so long as the dominant male doesn't perceive internal or external threats.

Genetics aside, it's amazing to see how similarly we operate as humans. In his 1967 book, Desmond Morris referred to us as *The Naked Ape*, and judging by our behavior, we fit the bill. We are generally clannish and social, led by aggressive males who, too often, try to impose their will through violent means. Although we share 99.9 percent of our DNA with every other of the nearly nine billion people on this planet, we none-the-less see our group as unique and often demonize others who we define as different from us. We go to war, maim, and kill one another, and try to gain territory from other groups. We callously justify our actions and commit unspeakable acts of violence, including on children and other vulnerable people. In this, we are little different from our cousins.

But chimpanzees aren't our only cousins. We are equally related to bonobos, a great ape that looks similar to a chimpanzee but lives in a different part of Africa. While bonobos also live in troops, they are led by coalitions of dominant females and are rarely violent. Bonobos are capable of altruism, compassion, empathy, kindness, and patience, exhibiting little aggression with each other. In fact, unfamiliar bonobos can freely mingle and cooperate with each other and are not territorial. Instead of fighting, bonobos engage in sexual activity to greet each other, form social bonds, resolve conflicts, and reconcile after disagreements. They literally make love, not war.

We resemble bonobos in some ways. We can cooperate and form coalitions, and sometimes resolve conflicts without violence. We show great kindness to others, as well as empathy, compassion, and altruism. As we look at our world today, we reflect both of our cousins, but generally, I wish we were less like chimpanzees and more like bonobos.

Chapter 40

The Rear-View Mirror

March 13

> *In tough times, we must remember that dawn will come, but we mustn't wait to find the light within and all around us.*

Remember the good old days? These days, it seems that many of us do, and in a wistful romanticized way. We long for the happy times we now miss and forget the misery that often rode alongside them. We seek to turn back the clock, imagining that we can have the benefits without the costs. But it doesn't work that way. Benefits always come with costs.

Russians longing for the glory of Soviet Union seem to have forgotten queuing in line for basic goods, speaking in hushed voices for fear of arrest, limits on travel and access to information, and a dismal economy. Yes, there was empire, but there was also oppression and poverty, gulags, defections. Americans seeking to make their country great again forget that their own ancestors were immigrants. They resent their government while benefiting from social security and farm subsidies. They don't know what it's like to be denied housing, work, or healthcare because of race, gender, disability, or national origin. Similarly, the United Kingdom severed ties with its largest trading partner, seeking to recreate Global Britain. Less remembered were the days in which their economy was known as the "sick man of Europe." Do they really miss having fewer goods in their stores and needing visas to work or study two hours away across the channel?

Rose-colored rear-view mirrors aren't limited to any nation, political ideology, religion, or social group. We vilify vaccines if we've never experienced a polio epidemic in our community. Dictatorship seems benign if we've never lived under one and seen our friends and relatives disappear to prison camps. Religious freedom, free speech, uncensored journalism, and unrestricted travel are devalued if we don't remember a time when we didn't have them.

It's easy to remember the comforts and forget the drawbacks of the past. The present is annoying! As we look at all the things that we don't like today, we fondly remember a time that never was. Life is hard and always has been, but we are much more attuned to the hardships we face currently and imagine that we can make them go away by turning back the clock.

By looking to the past, we lock ourselves into a mentality of scarcity. We hold onto what we have and stop imagining opportunities for growth. We view outsiders as competitors coming to steal what is rightfully ours rather than as collaborators and partners who can help us build a better future. We build walls and destroy bridges, listen only to ourselves, ignore facts we don't like, and inflict unspeakable cruelty and violence upon each other.

There is a reason we gaze forward through the windshield when we drive. If we keep looking back, we will eventually crash, and we will never see it coming. While we should learn about and from the past, there is no going back. The future is ahead of us, and that's where we must focus.

Chapter 41

Normal but Weird

March 24

> *Reality is what it is! It may be frustrating, uncomfortable, annoying, or undesirable. We might try to avoid it, pretend it's not really like that, wish for something else to happen, or hope that it changes miraculously. But in the end, reality doesn't care, and just stays as it is. If we can accept that and stare it in the eyes, we can assess our choices and start moving forward.*

Two years ago, our lives were normal, and we didn't even notice how normal they were, until a pandemic came and pointed it out to us. We did regular things like go to work, commute, eat out at restaurants, see movies, hang out with family and friends, and travel. We also took many extraordinary things for granted, like flying in the air to far-away places, moving underground through our cities, and gathering in huge numbers for entertainment.

Then, suddenly, everything changed. People got sick and hospitals filled up. Borders closed and flights got cancelled. First, we stopped shaking hands and instead touched elbows, and then we started washing our groceries from the store. We went into full lockdown, learned how to Zoom, tried to work with our kids on our laps while they went to school without ever leaving the house. Restaurants closed, busses ran empty, office buildings sat silent, and an eerie quiet settled over our cities.

Nothing was normal, and yet we adjusted. We started cooking and gardening, picked up new hobbies, met our neighbors outside, tried to hike and jog, and waited to see what the virus had in store. It came, and went, and came again in cycles, each with its own quirks and surprises. We sewed masks and developed vaccines, got tested and socially distanced, and learned how to make our lives work somehow despite the challenges we faced.

And then, the tide started turning. As more of us either got sick and recovered or got vaccinated and boosted, the number of new infections started waning. Each new variant seemed to be more contagious than the last but also less deadly, as the virus started moving from pandemic to endemic, from catastrophic to manageable.

We were tired of all of this and declared victory. "It's time to put the pandemic behind us and start living our lives again," came the cry from people around the globe. And so, we took off our masks and went back to the office, the bar, and the restaurant. We started meeting face to face, and spending more time back at work, and going to meetings, and sitting in traffic. Back to normal...but not really.

Many questions remained, and we entered an unusual time of transition - back at the office, but only some of us, and only some of the time, some in masks, others not. Some meetings in person, but others on Zoom. Life reverted almost back to what it was, but not quite. Life feels mostly normal, but weird, and weird feels like our new normal.

Chapter 42

Yes or No?

March 31

> *Many of us dislike conflict so much that even the possibility or the thought of conflict stops us from asserting our needs.*

Many of us say "yes" when people ask us to do things. Making others happy feels good, and we want to be liked. We want to be kind and helpful, and we enjoy the satisfaction of doing someone a favor. We also imagine that if we are agreeable all the time, then other people will appreciate our efforts and reward us in kind. Conversely, we sometimes say "yes" to avoid conflict, believing that "no" would only lead to confrontation. Whatever our reasoning, we often say "yes" when we should really be saying "no," and do so automatically.

But saying "yes" all the time also comes with downsides. Some requests are truly unreasonable and should be rejected. Sometimes people ask us to do things that are outside our scope of work, would take excessive time, or should be done by someone else, including them. Some requests are unfeasible, in the sense that we can't fulfill them even if we want to. If we say "yes" all the time, we eventually overcommit, become overwhelmed, work ourselves into the ground, and in the end, fail to deliver on our promises.

There are also emotional and social costs to saying "yes"

all the time. We might feel the dissonance when we recognize that we've just agreed to a request we should have refused. We might get angry or frustrated with our decision, judge ourselves harshly for agreeing, or worry about being seen as a pushover. We might feel resentful toward the other person for taking advantage of us or avoid interacting with them in the future. Unable to socialize or relax, we are perpetually exhausted, and despite our desire to please others and be fulfilled, we apologize all the time and feel hollow.

Our time and energy are finite, and we need to manage them carefully. By saying "yes" to everything, we abdicate our responsibility to ourselves and those in our care. Instead of managing our priorities strategically and paying closest attention to the most important matters, we try to do it all, and let ourselves and others down. We need to reframe how we think of the word "no" in our minds – we are not rejecting the other person but instead selecting the most valuable investment of our energy and time. There are always more things to do and more people to please, but by saying "no" to some things, we clear the space to focus on our highest priorities and have the greatest impact.

By worrying whether to say "yes" or "no" to a request, we're focusing on the wrong question. Instead of being guided by an internal compass based on fundamental values and strategic objectives, we define our actions through other people. "Yes" and "no" are both legitimate responses, so long as we say them for the right reasons, based on the things we value most, the relationships we cherish, and the accomplishments we wish to look back upon with pride.

Chapter 43

Inflation

April 3

> *When you don't have answers and can't see the way forward, it is easy to get paralyzed and stuck. Do something, anything, and at the very least, you will learn some things.*

We are in a period of rising inflation, and people are already feeling its impact. Everything is more expensive, and it's harder to make ends meet. Not being an economist, I can't give a full or accurate explanation of inflation, but I believe some of it comes down to supply and demand. When we want more things than we have, be it oil, food, employees, or computers, they start costing more. The bigger the difference between how much stuff we want and how much of it there is, the more inflation we can expect.

Of course, there's more to it than that, including the money supply, which can I think means the money available to governments, companies, and individuals to spend. If there is more money in the system, its value goes down, and once again, things start costing more. Governments manage the money supply by printing money, issuing bonds, setting interest rates, and other ways I don't completely understand. In the end, it feels like inflation is something that happens to us, without us having much say, and we must hope that our leaders have a better handle on it than we do.

But we do have some degree of influence if we choose to exercise it. If fuel costs are rising, we can look for ways to save energy. We can try to drive less, combine trips and carpool, ride bikes and walk, and use public transportation. Understandably, that's easier for some and very difficult for others, but overall, when energy was cheap, we bought big cars and squandered many opportunities to prepare ourselves for a time when it would cost more.

If cars and durable goods cost more now due to material and supply chain issues, we could try to hold off and wait to replace the ones we have. Again, easier for some than for others, but we have become accustomed to a lifestyle of rampant consumerism, addicted to buying things and throwing them away. We spent money we didn't have, got ourselves deep in debt, often buying things we didn't need and soon after didn't want any more. Now that governments are raising interest rates to lower inflation, some of our loans will also become more expensive to repay.

Individually, we may not have much influence over global or even national inflation, but we could exercise some control over the inflation that we experience personally. We can try to manage our discretionary expenses, lower our personal consumption, and work toward paying back our loans, starting with the most expensive ones. Each of our actions may be small, but if enough of us try, we can impact the big picture as well. As is often the case, we can choose whether to view ourselves as victims and look for someone to blame or be proactive and take the actions within our power. Our behavior helped cause today's inflation, and if we wish to overcome it, we need to be part of the solution.

Chapter 44

Optimism and the End of Humanity

April 12

> *Success is never certain, but failure is also not preordained. We're always in a game of odds, so if we make the best choices we can and fortune smiles upon us, we can and should hope for the best.*

In seventy thousand years, our species has gone from wandering about the savannas of Africa to dominating the planet and venturing beyond. We've come so far in such a short time, that it's hard to remember how fragile we really are. We can only survive on one planet and within very limited conditions, and although there are several billions of us now, we're always under threat of extinction. After all, the Earth has been around for a few billion years, and during that time, species have come and gone, and there is every reason to think that, someday, we might go the same way.

There are lots of threats to our survival. Earth could be struck by an asteroid or blasted by gamma rays, super-volcanos can poison our atmosphere, or devastating pathogens could decimate our population. Some of the mass extinction events in our planet's history eliminated over ninety percent of the species that existed at the time, and there is no guarantee that we would be spared if another were to happen.

But, if that's not scary enough, we seem to be trying to do ourselves in. We've pumped so much carbon dioxide and methane into the atmosphere that our planet is warming. We've made our home less livable through deforestation, water and air pollution, nuclear waste, and landfills. We have destroyed ecosystems and ushered in another great extinction event, this time caused by our very presence and our impact on our surroundings, killing off numerous species, including some, like bees, that are critical to our survival.

More directly, armed conflicts directly kill tens of thousands every year, and homicide, both criminal and interpersonal, even more. Millions are displaced and many people die from illness and hunger, accidents, and exposure. Poverty and income inequality, coupled with the politics of corruption and greed, cause misery and death. In addition, we possess enough nuclear warheads to guarantee our extinction, with more countries trying to join the club each year, as well as chemical and biological weapons that, if used, could go out of control and kill us all. Finally, we are developing technologies in robotics and artificial intelligence that threaten the very definition of our humanity.

Despite, or perhaps because of these things, we have reason to remain optimistic. Our odds of getting to where we are today were never great, yet here we are. Some of the threats to our survival are too big for us to worry about, and, as for the awful things we do to each other and the planet, there is a lot of good with the bad. Kindness and empathy face up to cruelty and aggression; resourceful innovation tackles the consequences of our bad choices. The end is always near, but we can never give up hope. We are an adaptable species and have been lucky thus far. Let us choose optimism and hope to keep going a bit longer.

Chapter 45

What Do We Know?

April 16

> *Speak with courage and kindness, listen with curiosity and empathy, and disagree without being disagreeable.*

We think we know many things, but if pressed, would be unable to demonstrate that we really know them. As Philip Fernback said in his TEDxMileHigh talk called "Why do we believe things that aren't true," the amount of factual information that our brains can retain is remarkably small. To compensate, we supplement our actual knowledge with social knowledge. Rather than investigate and retain facts on our own, we rely on information and interpretation from other people, and in doing so, vastly increase our effective knowledge base.

This is not necessarily a bad thing, as it allows us to contemplate ideas and make decisions beyond our capacity as individuals. In *Sapiens*, Yuval Harari also extols our ability to collaborate flexibly and in large numbers, by communicating ideas and collectively believing them. According to Harari, this is key to our success as a species, even if the ideas we communicate and share are largely invented by us.

But every coin has two sides, and just as our reliance on social knowledge makes us powerful, it also puts us in danger. If much of what we think we know comes not from our own scientific investigation of the world around us but instead from repeating ideas generated by other people, then our perception of the world becomes extremely vulnerable to our social context. What we see is therefore less a product of our eyes than of the voices whispering in our ears, and we are pressured to listen to those voices. In the words of Groucho Marx, "Who you gonna believe, me or your lying eyes?"

According to Jonathan Haidt, in *The Righteous Mind*, we are also "groupish," in that we are more likely to believe people like ourselves, and in addition, we are prone to the confirmatory bias of seeing and remembering what we already believe from before. We can therefore convince ourselves to regard pretty much any information as factual, so long as it's consistent with what we believe already and is delivered to us by a trusted voice from within our group, especially if this "fact" is then repeated by others.

These days, we are bombarded by overwhelming amounts of information, and few of us have the ability or time to sort through it. We therefore rely on partisan news sources, social media, and trusted friends to help us interpret the world, and are increasingly vulnerable to misinformation and manipulation. While our friends might inadvertently mislead us, other, less ethical actors purposely try to make us believe "alternative facts" that suit their interests, sometimes to our own detriment. As Carl Sagan warned us in *The Demon Haunted World*, we need to improve our ability to think like scientists and question what others tell us. As a start, we must accept the notion that we often don't really know what we think we know and keep an open mind to other ideas. What do we know? Not as much as we believe.

Chapter 46

The Passage of Time

May 12

> *Life's not fair, nor is it unfair. It just is, and we must cherish it with all its ups and downs, joys and heartbreaks.*

When my father turned seventy, I asked him if it felt weird, and he replied, "less weird than having my son turn forty." Time, like everything else we encounter, is partly real and partly perception, and both are important.

The reality of time is that it keeps moving along, and so far, anyway, only forward. I can't stop the clock, nor do I control the ending of a day or the passage of one year to the next. That conversation with my dad is itself almost two decades in the past, and it strikes me that soon I might be on the other end of a similar conversation with one of my kids.

But time is also impacted by perception, at times standing still while at other times racing by. To this day, on a long trip, I still think, "are we there yet?" as the minutes crawl by and it feels like the drive will never end. Some meetings, classes, and Zoom calls also make time seem to slow down. On the other hand, anything fun ends too soon, and we feel like we've just gotten started. The days might feel long, but the years pass by quickly.

Nowhere is the passage of time clearer to me than in observing the people I love and the places I cherish. My mother died sixteen years ago today, and the last of my grandparents over thirty years ago. My friends are starting to retire, their kids are having children, and my former students are now older than I was when I was teaching them. My own kids have grown into young adults, and I can't think of them as I did before when they were little children. Whether I feel like time is moving slowly or rushing by, one day follows the next, and every moment happens only once, disappearing into history to make room for the one that follows.

It's tempting to look back upon the past with nostalgia, longing for days gone by or people that I miss, and I might get very wistful or sad. While I treasure the positive memories I've built and keep my loved ones in my heart, I must also stay present in the moment and look forward to the future rather than retreat into the past. For one thing, the past wasn't all wonderful, and it's unproductive to try to reconstruct it based on selective recollection. In addition, the world has changed since then, and try as I might, any attempt at going backward will ultimately fail.

My mother's untimely death reminds me that the future is unknowable, and that while we need to prepare for tomorrow, we must live our lives today. This is our moment, and we need to pay attention to it before it disappears. Time passes, and our portion of it is limited. That's not our choice. What we do with it matters, and it helps to be reminded of that once in a while.

Chapter 47

Never Good Enough

May 15

> *Things don't always turn out the way we want, but that's okay. Sometimes disappointments usher in new opportunities, as we understand the narrow nature of our earlier aspirations and discover possibilities we didn't even know to look for.*

Some of us go through life feeling like whatever we accomplish, however hard we work, no matter how much praise we get, we're never good enough. We always have to try harder, do better, tackle the next challenge, climb a higher mountain, and yet when we get to the summit, we still feel inadequate and ask what's next. We downplay our successes, take our accomplishments for granted, and trivialize our triumphs. Conversely, we wallow in our failures till they define our life experience and dent our self-esteem.

Consequently, we feel like inadequate imposters, terrified that someone will find us out. If a job interview goes well, we think that "we pulled the wool over their eyes," or if someone likes us, we think "that's because they don't really know us yet." If we get an "A" on an exam, we feel like we were lucky that the teacher asked easy questions, or if someone praises our performance, we think "they're just being nice and not telling me what they really think." We live our lives like hunted animals, scurrying from hiding place to hiding place, terrified and out of breath.

If this is our experience, we don't feel good about much, and we're not having any fun. We weave a narrative of failure and inadequacy about ourselves and use every experience to reinforce this narrative. We see and interpret the world through a distorted lens in which we can't do anything right, and if anything goes well, it is by accident, while anything that doesn't go well confirms that we are, indeed, losers. No wonder we're so anxious all the time. We put tremendous pressure on ourselves to succeed but are always doomed to fail in our own judgment.

Why do we do this? After all, we have the choice to look at things any way we want. How do we benefit from being so harsh and unkind to ourselves? Why can't we enjoy our accomplishments and celebrate our successes? Why must we judge ourselves at all rather than accept that like everyone else? We embody a mix of characteristics and simply are who we are.

Some of this derives from messaging we are given by others, and over time, make our own. Our families, society, and surroundings shape who we are, what we do, and how we evaluate ourselves. In addition, feeling inadequate is emotionally safer than expecting to achieve and risking failure. If we already believe ourselves to be imposters, then no one can make us feel worse than we already feel. We can't disappoint if we have no expectations of achieving anything of note.

But a life defined by fear is a life diminished. To build up our self-confidence, we can take small risks, observe, log the results, ask for feedback, and get support from people we trust. Over time, we can become the authors rather than the victims of our narratives, shape our life experience, and leave the imposter behind.

Chapter 48

Where to Begin

May 20

> *When things are frustrating us, instead of pushing harder, we should try to see what's getting in the way. We can be more effective by focusing on removing barriers rather than by using more brute force.*

When faced with several tasks, some more challenging, some less, should we start with the easy ones or tackle the most difficult ones first? If we start with the easy tasks, we might get tired or take too long before getting to the hard ones, even if they are more important. Conversely, if we start with the hardest, we might get stuck and give up, or might take so much time that we leave other, more doable matters, untouched.

Similarly, when approaching a multi-issue conflict, should we negotiate the most intractable issues first? Does it make sense to agree upon minor issues only to go back to square one because we couldn't resolve the big ones. At the same time, we might have an easier time dealing with the most difficult issues if we've gotten to know each other by negotiating the easier ones first. It might feel encouraging for us to practice notching some wins upon our belts and increase our confidence and resolve when we approach the tough areas of contention.

Like many questions, this one has no simple answer, though different people prefer one method over the other. Some of us get too anxious leaving the hard tasks or intractable differences to the end and try instead to take matters head-on, toughing it out from the outset with the hope that things will get easier over time. If we do get stumped by too tough an issue right away, we console ourselves by noting that at least we didn't waste a lot of time before we found out matters were hopeless.

Others of us get overwhelmed when faced with the impossible task or insurmountable conflict. We prefer to get some small wins out of the way to feel some progress and lift our spirits before trying to get our arms around the tougher ones. We love to cross things off our checklists, and the more items we've put behind us, the more confident we feel moving forward.

Of course, there are other methods as well. We could decide to address matters in chronological order, based on when they came to our attention, or by priority, based on when they are due. We could pick an arbitrary rule, such as alphabetical order, or simply throw darts at our list and let random selection decide the order.

Ultimately, every one of these approaches could work, and yet they might also equally fail. To tackle multiple issues, we might instead want to adopt a flexible approach, based on the specific nature of the matters at hand, our priorities in the situation, the preferences of our partners, our mood or mindset, and other factors. We could also try one method, assess our success, and possibly choose a different approach if we don't like the results. By being purposeful and flexible rather than dogmatic, we are likely to be more successful in a variety of situations and more resilient in the face of adversity.

Chapter 49

Ripples

May 30

> *When the music stops and the dancing is over, what wisps of joy and connection remain, uplifting our spirits through the long days that follow?*

I went sea kayaking yesterday, paddling in the beautiful waters near Plum Island in Massachusetts for over five hours. It was glorious! Perfect weather, sunny but not too hot, calm seas and barely any wind. The water was so clear that we could see the sunlight dancing on the ocean floor at quite some depth. Sea birds, from ospreys to herons and seagulls, terns, and cormorants, accompanied us as we crossed open water, hugged the beaches, meandered through salt marshes, and explored rocky inlets.

Later that evening, working at my desk, cooking in the kitchen, or sitting down for dinner, I kept feeling my body swaying side to side, still responding to the rocking of the waves in the ocean. After bobbing on the tides for all those hours, the feeling of motion persisted long after I was safely on dry land, and it got me thinking of the ways in which past events send ripples into our ongoing experience.

Yesterday's trip is gone, relegated to the past and preserved only in photos, memories, or stories. That happened the moment we pulled the boats from the water. But the sensation of motion, an involuntary response to our environment, continued for hours till it faded overnight. We all carry our past experiences with us as we go about our lives. Traumatic or difficult events can provoke stress reactions that can last a lifetime for some people, scarring over but never disappearing entirely. Conversely, moments of elation also linger. The warm memory of a first kiss, a goal achieved, a discovery shared with another, can sustain us even as we move on to new things.

All things fade with time, as new events and experiences flood our conscious minds with new stimuli, but some sensations continue to impact us, subconsciously shaping how we react and approach the world around us. If we pay attention, we can notice the rocking motion generated by these feelings and make deliberate choices regarding how to respond to them. While the ripples may be involuntary and subconscious, we can learn to be mindful and aware of what they are and how they impact our feelings and behavior. We can then try to reinforce the positive responses and diminish the ones that make life more difficult.

What voices are we listening to when we turn our attention inward? Are we focusing on our successes, remembering that we are capable and worthy, or on our failures, reinforcing our negative narratives? What images do we see when we shut our eyes and connect with our past? Are we seeing ourselves at our best, painted in bright colors on a sunny background, or do we gravitate to our darker moments, beaten down by events, disappointed and dejected? It's all there, rippling under the surface, and our choice is to decide where to explore and what to emphasize. Kayaking trips are fleeting and finite, but the feeling persists, helping me smile as I face a new day.

Chapter 50

A Quiet Day

June 7

> *The news changes every day, but in many ways, it stays remarkably consistent over time. Some of us are drawn to it, hanging on every new word, hoping and dreading. Others of us let it slide by unnoticed, lulled by our complacency or simply uninterested. Somewhere between those two extremes there is a healthy place, neither ignoring the news nor obsessing about it.*

I long for a quiet day in which I turn on the news, and the biggest story is so inconsequential that I sigh in relief and go about my business. It's been eons since I've felt that way, and it's more likely that I peek at the news with trepidation, bracing myself for the next stressful event. New crises erupt long before their predecessors have subsided, elevating our collective experience to one of near-constant anxiety. We wonder what's coming next while still processing the trauma of recent events.

Some of us have become numb or have stopped looking at the news altogether. Yes, thousands are dying, and millions have been displaced in a brutal war, but all that is far away, so we focus on making a living and tending our gardens. Even if we were engaged several months ago, when the violence erupted, it's difficult for us to remain as interested in the war, and we move on to other crises, while the devastation continues.

Sadly, there is no shortage of new matters to draw our attention. Mass shootings make headlines nearly every week—first a store, then a school and a hospital, in addition to numerous other shootings and acts of violence. No wonder we feel unsafe, bracing ourselves for the next tragedy while our polarized society and government solve nothing.

On the health front, after over two years of near-constant pandemic news, we are desperate to move on, only to be hit with monkeypox. Who knew that was even a thing, but now it's all over the internet. The economic news isn't any less stressful, as inflation makes it harder to pay the bills, supply chain problems constrain production, more companies announce layoffs while others struggle to find workers.

Can't we just talk about the weather? Unfortunately, climate change has made even looking at the forecast more daunting. Australia is under water, California is parched, New Mexico is on fire, the glaciers are disappearing, and violent storms are headed our way. Why is the news so stressful now? Perhaps cable news and social media have made us hyper-aware of the world's tragedies, amplifying crises to get our attention. Could it be that things have always been this way, or that much of this is fake news, made up by the media?

Or maybe all of this bad news is a warning, a cautionary tale, that as our numbers have grown and the Earth has gotten more crowded, our margin of error has shrunk, and we must pay more attention to what we are doing or suffer the consequences. We deserve quiet days, but we are unlikely to get them unless we learn to treat each other and the world around us with greater empathy and kindness, and to tolerate less division and bad behavior from our fellow humans.

Chapter 51

Money

June 12

> *Your narrative defines your life experience, so be mindful of what you are telling yourself.*

Many of us get uncomfortable when talking about money, especially for our own benefit. We are happy to discuss the great services we provide our clients but squirm when we have to bring up the fee. We interview well but then avoid negotiating the starting salary. But why does money make us so squeamish?

One challenge is that money often determines where we can live, our healthcare and education choices, and what we can afford to buy. That fact alone raises our anxiety level, since we know that if things don't go well, our lives might be constrained. We imagine money negotiations to be win-lose, in that any money we negotiate for ourselves must be a loss for the other person. Money negotiations therefore feel unpleasant, adversarial, and competitive, raising our fear regarding how the other person might respond.

Money can also tie into how we feel about ourselves. We admire billionaires for no other reason than that they have a lot of money and look down upon people who have less. We even use the phrase "what is he worth?" when discussing how much money someone has. While there should be no connection between money and self-worth, societal norms make it hard for us to break that link in our minds. Thus, when we negotiate financial matters, emotionally we are negotiating our personal value, and that's terribly stressful.

What makes it even harder is that we don't always get what we want. If we ask for a ten percent raise but are offered two percent, is our boss telling us that we are not as good as we think we are? Are we inadequate at advocating for ourselves? Did we fail? As I discuss in *Collywobbles: How to Negotiate When Negotiating Makes You Nervous*, rejection is never fun but being rejected in money negotiations can feel particularly painful, because it ties into how we feel about ourselves.

Money negotiations also often take place on an uneven playing field. When we ask for a raise, the boss has positional power over us in the organization. When we ask a client for a fee, we know that the client can go somewhere else. Being on the wrong end of a power imbalance can make us feel less confident to advocate for our needs, and we are more likely to back down or avoid negotiating entirely.

Finally, some of us were taught that money is dirty and bringing it up is unseemly. If money was never discussed or negotiated in front of us, how could we learn how to engage with it? To increase our capacity to negotiate over money, we need to first understand our emotional reaction to it and then to practice negotiating financial matters until we become more comfortable, taking small risks initially and becoming bolder over time.

Chapter 52

Up, Up and Away

June 15

> *Some of our most interesting journeys are unexpected. We go about our routines, unaware that an unusual turn of events is just around the corner. By letting the road take us where it may, we break through our limitations and enrich our lives.*

I'm on an airplane today! Two and a half years ago, I was on a plane nearly every week, flying around the globe. Today, however, this flight is noteworthy, as I am taking my first post-pandemic flight. On one hand, it's remarkable how routine it was, from the ride to the airport, though security, boarding, and onto the flight. On the other, it was odd to observe my state of mind.

Packing took me significantly longer than it used to. Before, I'd always have a carry-on ready, my toiletries in a Ziploc, and my work bag preloaded with the essentials. Packing meant gathering a few specific items and then choosing what clothes to bring along. Half an hour maximum! This time, it took me hours to even find the various things I needed, and I had to keep a running list of items I didn't want to forget. The process felt inefficient, awkward, and anxiety-provoking, as if I was using the wrong hand the whole time. My brain was rusty, and I felt clunky.

While everything about the trip was normal, none of it

felt normal after two years of being away. I kept waiting for something to go wrong on the way to the airport, going through security, finding the gate, and boarding the flight. Nothing did, but it was hard to let go of the anticipatory anxiety. Some things had changed since the last time I flew, mostly in a negative direction. I'd heard of flight cancellations, bad behavior by passengers, long lines at security, and other problems. I also kept worrying that I'd forgotten something and that whatever it was, would disrupt my trip in some way.

Over the past two and a half years, I'd turned into a homebody, mostly staying within about twenty miles of my hometown. I'd grown comfortable in the small and the local and grew fearful of stepping outside my bubble. On the positive side, my garden is beautiful, and I discovered delightful corners of my neighborhood that I never knew existed. On the other hand, my horizons had shrunk, and the rest of the world had gotten scary. I'm glad to be up in the air again. It's good for me.

I started thinking about the danger of living insular lives, limited to the local and familiar. I've had the benefit of traveling the world, but for many people their experience of other people and places is limited to hearsay and assumptions. It's easy to fear or dislike others if we only know them through television or social media. Once beyond the bubble, we quickly realize that people are much the same everywhere, trying to make a living, raise their families, and find happiness and fulfilment. By going out into the world, we lose our fear and discover wonders, without diminishing our love of home. Now, it's time to sit back, relax, and enjoy the flight.

Chapter 53

The Tides

June 24

> *Progress isn't linear and success isn't constant. There are moments of triumph followed by devastating setbacks, and many days when nothing seems to happen at all. All we can do is to put one foot in front of the other, try to make the best decisions we can, and persevere.*

As a kid, I loved building sandcastles on the beach and fighting the waves as the tide rolled back in. No matter how much sand I added, how many protective moats and walls I constructed, or how cleverly I designed my castle, eventually the ocean would win, destroying everything I'd built. But then, the tide would crest, the ocean would recede, and I'd build an even better castle on the flat, wet sand. Tides come and go, and the ocean is much bigger than I am. I like fighting the good fight, feel humbled by the power of the sea, and am calmed by the cyclical nature of things.

We live in treacherous times, and many people fear that the important works we have built as a species are imperiled. Democracy is in retreat all over the world, autocrats are solidifying their grip on power, and dissent is crushed in cruel and brutal ways. In too many places, military force is used to settle conflicts, killing thousands, displacing millions, and throwing entire regions into poverty. Political corruption, civil liberties, income inequality, violence, drug overdoses, and other societal ills all seem to be on the rise, while kindness, empathy, and tolerance are becoming more difficult to find.

It feels like the very fabric of society is coming apart, as we vilify and demonize each other on social media, fanning distrust and hatred of people we define as others. We only read what we already believe and believe what people in our own circle tell us, reinforcing all our stereotypes, prejudices, and biases. We've become less worldly, more ignorant, and more insular, mindlessly repeating falsehoods we picked up in memes, videos, and tweets. We're becoming a lesser version of ourselves.

The news is distressing, more bad than good, and even if we get the occasional uplifting tale, for the most part, we are overwhelmed by a torrent of scary and disappointing stories. Climate change is causing our planet to burn in some places and drown in others, crops are failing, and severe storms tear apart our homes. Covid-19 has killed and sickened millions around the world, and before we can catch our breath, monkeypox is on the rise. The economy is in tatters, inflation is rising, and social injustice is becoming more extreme. No wonder we're anxious and depressed.

And none of this is stopping soon. Things can get a lot worse before they start getting better. It feels like the tide is rising, and soon, all the things we value and cherish will be swept away. This may be. Humanity has done this to itself before, and times got really awful. But, each time, eventually the tide receded, and we rebuilt even better than before. As we face the tide of pain and destruction ahead, we need to work with all our will to salvage what we can of our humanity, but also take solace in the cycles of the tides.

Chapter 54

Not So Simple

July 2

> *It may be difficult to accept reality sometimes but far more dangerous to ignore it or invent imaginary facts of our own choosing.*

Summer is upon us once again, and this, the third summer since Covid-19 first made it into the headlines, feels different. The world has largely gone back to normal. People are traveling again, going back to the office, stuck in traffic, eating at restaurants, and getting together with friends and family. In much of life, people are talking about the Covid pandemic in the past tense and, if anything, saying that we need to accept it as endemic, no different from the common cold or flu.

Except that the reality is not so simple. As I write these words, my wife is in bed, isolating with Covid, and has been there for a week with a headache, sore throat, cough, joint pain, and chills. I've been staying away, trying not to catch it myself, and our house has been bisected into the Covid zone and the living zone. The disruption to our lives has been significant, even though we are fortunate compared to many who've had to deal with the disease under far more difficult conditions. Yes, it's like the flu, in some ways, but more disruptive in others.

Meanwhile, I tried to get together with a colleague the other night but couldn't, because he was still recovering from Covid. My sister-in-law also had it recently and took weeks to get better. Kids have been sent home from schools and camps, impacting their parents' ability to work, travel plans have had to be cancelled last-minute due to positive test results, and return-to-normal has quickly turned into get-back-in-bed-and-isolate for many people.

All this is to say is that while Covid has transformed and transitioned over the past few months, it can still impact our lives in significant ways. Whether we think the pandemic is over, still among us, or somewhere in between, more people are getting sick, hospitalizations are going up, and life isn't quite back to normal. We are living in a liminal time, neither locked down nor normal, in the office but not, together but wary, mostly healthy but not entirely. It is a time of transition and uncertainty, and therefore stress. Anytime we don't know where we stand, we get more anxious, and this feeling has been with us for a long time already.

The healthiest way forward involves caring for each other with empathy. We must accept that different people will respond differently to these circumstances and keep an open mind with the people we understand the least and disagree with the most. We need to support each other even as we argue and debate the best way forward. Stressful times can be divisive, and these are no exception. How we come out of them through to the other side will depend upon our ability to unite and move beyond our divisions.

Chapter 55

The Bystander Effect

July 9

Who are you, and what do you stand for?

The 1964 murder and rape of Kitty Genovese, and subsequent reporting in the New York Times claiming that 38 people witnessed the attack and didn't intervene, spawned the term *the bystander effect*. While the account of the attack was inaccurate, the bystander effect turned out to be real, asserting that bystanders are less likely to help someone in need, even in an emergency, if other people are present, or even if they imagine others to be nearby.

When we witness someone in distress, we are presented with the dilemma of whether to intervene and potentially put ourselves at risk, or to keep walking. To intervene, we must first notice that something is wrong, define the situation as requiring help, determine that we are personally responsible, figure out what to do, and then act. We are more likely to act if helping the other person makes us feel better about ourselves or avoid the guilt of having not helped and are less likely to act if we fear negative consequences to ourselves as a result of intervening.

Many other factors impact whether we will help a stranger in distress, but one thing is certain – over the course of our lives, we will encounter people in trouble and will have to decide what, if anything, to do about it. As a species, our record isn't stellar in this regard. Most of us watch the brutal Russian invasion of Ukraine with horror, but neither do anything ourselves nor urge our governments to do anything about it. We did the same when Russia obliterated Grozny and flattened Aleppo.

We looked on when Myanmar attacked and displaced the Rohingya, as China represses the Uyghurs, and when Hutus attacked Tutsis in Rwanda. Our bystander apathy isn't limited to wars but also when we witness oppression, political violence, ethnic cleansing, disease, hunger, and other calamities. Some people act, but most of us don't. Some of us don't care, others feel helpless, some are scared, and others feel it's not our place to intervene.

While it's not our role to judge whether someone should have intervened or not, the result of this global bystander effect is that horrible things continue to happen all over the world. This isn't new, but with today's video and communication technology, we can no longer claim to be unaware. We can't be expected to fix everything in the world but tolerating this much horror without taking some action is wrong and will eventually backfire.

To quote Pastor Martin Niemöller regarding Nazi Germany, "First they came for the socialists, and I did not speak out—because I was not a socialist. Then they came for the trade unionists, and I did not speak out— because I was not a trade unionist. Then they came for the Jews, and I did not speak out—because I was not a Jew. Then they came for me—and there was no one left to speak for me."

Chapter 56

Lies and Illusions

July 20

> *It's your choice whether to believe in gravity or not, but gravity doesn't care. If you ignore it, you will fall down the stairs and get hurt regardless of what you choose to believe.*

We know so little, and the little that we do know, if we don't like, we dismiss out of hand. Rather than investigating facts, we lie to ourselves and to others and live in a world of illusion fabricated by our imaginations. Instead of going to the effort of finding out real facts and calibrating our narratives using actual information, we find it easier to create stories out of whole cloth, so long as they conform to what we already believe.

This has always been. Despite overwhelming evidence that the Earth is round, many people still believe that it is flat and concoct elaborate explanations as to why it appears spherical from space. After we sent people to the moon, some refused to believe that the moon landing was real and came up with complex conspiracy theories as to what had really happened. No matter the subject, some of us turn away from the investigation of the facts and prefer to imagine an alternative reality.

At this point in history, social media has given unprecedented voice to these narratives, providing a platform for stories and lies to spread and mutate and making it hard to discern reality from illusion. Not knowing what to believe and lacking the skills to find out for ourselves, we've come to rely on our social network for confirmation. If we can't believe our eyes and don't know how to determine the truth, believing someone we trust feels like the best we can do.

As a result, we have become factionalized and divided, believing different prophets and increasingly unable to think for ourselves. Regarding our health, we listen to politicians we admire rather than to doctors who've studied the science. We make financial decisions based on memes and use online videos as classrooms without knowing whether the creators of those videos are knowledgeable or truthful. We've become complacent and lazy regarding our sources and verifying our facts.

The line between reality and fiction becomes blurrier daily. Soon, deep fake videos and AI might make it impossible for us to determine what's real. At that point, any lie or story will be as good as the truth, putting immense power in the hands of those who control the narratives. Do we really want to live at the mercy of propaganda machines, corporate spin doctors, or any individual with a computer and an agenda?

Without the ability to discern facts, we run the risk of sleepwalking into disaster because we've imagined that everything's fine. We'll miss the danger signs and dismiss warnings as lies, only to look back in dismay when things have gone too far. Instead of repeating stories from others, we need to ask hard questions, research the facts, and think for ourselves. We are a resourceful and resilient species, but we can also be self-destructive. We must therefore use our imaginations to build a future based on reality rather than just invent stories that make ourselves feel better.

Chapter 57

Feeling the Heat

July 26

> *Some people can't stand the winter when the weather gets too cold. Others suffer during the summer when it gets too hot. Nearly everyone complains when the humidity is high. And yet humans have thrived in all these conditions for hundreds of thousands of years. We are adaptable in our bodies, and if we can learn to be equally flexible in our minds, we too can thrive.*

We are in the middle of a heat wave. As the temperature grows uncomfortable, I am tempted to open the refrigerator and stand in front of it. It's nice and cool in my fridge, so my intuition says that opening the fridge door would also cool me and my house. While I might feel a bit cooler for a few minutes as the dissipating cold from the fridge blows out into my kitchen, the longer I stand there, the warmer my house would get. The physics of refrigeration would cause my fridge to use more energy and radiate heat into my kitchen. In the end, my intuition based on limited and localized data is inaccurate, and without understanding the underlying science, I draw the wrong conclusions.

Globally, it's tempting to address the misery and hardship caused by the hotter weather through increased access to air conditioning, and it would certainly help a great many people. But just like my fridge, air conditioners produce heat as they cool, venting that heat outside and using large quantities of electricity. Since most electricity worldwide is generated through the burning of fossil fuels, in the end, individual rooms or buildings become cooler while the world overall continues to get warmer.

Our focus on attending to our immediate and personal concerns even if our actions harm us in the long term or create global problems isn't unique to cooling ourselves during a heat wave. Through millennia of evolution, we have been programmed to take care of ourselves first, then our small family or social group, then our tribe or nation, then our species, and finally the rest of the planet. This hierarchy worked out well hundreds of years ago, when our population was a small fraction of what it is currently, and we were dispersed into small clans separated by vast expanses of wilderness.

We've also been programmed to respond to our senses and to take immediate action to protect ourselves. Dating back to our hunter-gatherer days when we were chased by predators, our ability to understand and react to our immediate surroundings was a survival skill. It was okay for us to misunderstand cause and effect so long as we knew how to act in the moment.

But things have changed. With our population closing on eight billion, having nearly tripled in the past fifty years, we have come to dominate the planet and push its resources to capacity. All our choices, from the food we eat to the homes we build, our social and political structures, and the way we use energy, now carry global repercussions and come back to haunt us sooner than we expect. We can no longer afford to act selfishly and locally and need to understand the science surrounding our decisions. The alternative is global misery, as heat waves, famines, floods, fires, and wars dominate our news. We must accept that opening the fridge is an illusion, and work instead to find real, fact-based solutions.

Chapter 58

Always Negotiating

July 31

> *Conflict amplifies our fear of losing everything, of damaging our relationships, and of emotional pain, but fear of conflict is also dangerous. We become so cautious that we fail to speak our minds and don't engage in meaningful debate. We need to take some risks, build trust, and advocate for our ideas while listening to others.*

It's hard to read the news these days! There's a bloody war in Ukraine, and that's one of over two dozen conflicts in the world today. Domestically, people of different politics and ideologies demonize each other, each vying to reshape their countries in a different image. Companies engage in battle with each other, and as the economy and climate fall apart on us, we fight over the very meaning of facts, data, and truth. Why is there so much fighting and so little negotiation to resolve these disputes?

When a conflict erupts, it's not always certain whether it will be resolved by force or through negotiation. This is true whether we're talking about an international conflict over borders and territory, a commercial conflict between two corporations, or an interpersonal conflict between family members. As the parties square off against each other we wonder what they will do. Will they try to talk and come to a mutually acceptable solution, or will they take unilateral actions, recruit allies, and fight? But in fact, everything is part of a greater negotiation in which people calculate the risks and benefits of different actions and go in different directions as circumstances require.

Every negotiation takes place in the shadow of the alternatives available to each party. When negotiating with a distributor to sell our products, we also evaluate the market opportunity, interview other distributors, and consider selling our products directly. If we find a better or cheaper alternative, we need this distributor less, and therefore have a stronger hand in the negotiation.

In territorial matters between nations, most conflicts do eventually get settled through negotiation, because the cost of winning outright is generally too high for either side to bear; however, there is often a period of conflict whose purpose is to put either side at a competitive advantage during the final negotiations. During this time, the nations might engage in diplomatic maneuvers to recruit allies or leverage political, economic, and military pressure.

It's helpful to think of both the conflict and the negotiation process together as part of a greater whole. This gives us a better chance of resolving the matter with less pain and bloodshed. It's not helpful to think of one course of action as good and the other as bad, since they are generally linked in the minds of the disputants. As we look around the world today, there is quite a bit of conflict. If we want to move humanity away from the use of force and toward more peaceful conflict resolution, we need to see the alternatives through the eyes of both parties and take action to make unilateral moves less palatable and negotiated solutions more likely.

Chapter 59

The Sandcastle

August 8

> *Life is how we look at it, and the more we slow down, look around us, savor the little things, focus on the positives, and appreciate everything we have, the better our experience. Life can be challenging and hard. That's not up to us. But life is also good, if only we choose to make it so.*

On the shore, past the turning of the tide, I came upon a lonely sandcastle fighting bravely against the sea battering its walls relentlessly in a cascade of ever-higher waves. Whoever had built it designed it to last, reinforcing its walls with large seashells and adorning it with tall towers and sturdy ramparts. For a few moments, it seemed to work, as at first, the spent surf barely tickled the castle's foundations. Over time, as the water rose and the waves became more fearsome, the mighty castle began to crumble.

First, the walls began eroding from the bottom, ever-more concave, topped by cantilevered overhangs clinging precariously to the sandy parapets. Then, ominous cracks started to form, as the outer walls separated from the main structure, eventually succumbing to the never-ending hammering of the waves. As the water climbed further up the beach, the castle was encircled, its sands swept away by the waters rushing back to sea, a forlorn holdout of human endeavor in a vast and immensely powerful ocean. One by one, the ramparts tumbled, the walls cracked and fell to their doom, until the castle was overrun completely, gone from memory.

I stood, as if riveted to the beach, fascinated by the drama of sand and water. This scene, versions of which have been playing out on Earth for billions of years, reminded me that like the sandcastle, our lives are fleeting, and a mere turning of the tide can wash us away, out of action, and soon forgotten. Is everything so temporary and pointless? If, in the end, we are nothing more than sandcastles, nothing we do really matters. Our hopes and dreams die with us, and even as we live, our days are spent resisting the inevitable tide of time, pushing off the day when we, too, are erased from existence.

And yet, I was also struck by the incredible beauty of the scene, every drop of water and grain of sand telling a story. Who were the builders, now long gone, their souls etched temporarily onto the beach? Would they return to check on their creation? Would they be sad to see it obliterated? As I gazed upon the destruction of their handiwork, their story became mine, and now, through these words, yours. Long after the sandcastle's demise, and even after I, too, have succumbed to the inevitable, the story might live on.

Meanwhile, we live and must celebrate each moment, enjoying the ocean breeze, rejoicing as the cool waves splash at our ankles, cherishing the sound of surf and gull, and watching in fascination as the tale of sand and water unfolds before our eyes. In the end, the ocean always wins, taking back what it has given. But in the small space between creation and loss is our moment, frozen in time, and if we pause and pay attention, we are rewarded with a glimpse of the eternal.

Chapter 60

Go Away!

August 15

> *Occasionally, we might want to inventory our habits to determine whether they are still serving us or if we have begun to serve them. Once aware, we have the choice of which to keep and which to drop and can then embark on the difficult task of changing our ways.*

I come from a nomadic tradition in which much was temporary, and the world was a big, big place. For generations, my family lived in multiple countries on different continents, and travel was as normal to us as walking to the store, all while maintaining our connections and traditions. As an adult, I traveled extensively for work, spanning four continents, encountering new people and cultures, learning constantly, and having great fun in the process.

Then, the pandemic descended upon us and we locked down at home. For over two years, my world was limited to the close and the familiar, and that, too, became wonderful, but in a different way. Local parks became my travel destinations, local streets my highways, the garden my forest, and the kitchen my amusement park. I walked the same well-trodden paths daily and never ventured farther out from home than a car could take me in a leisurely day trip. My experience became smaller, as the wide world receded in distance and faded from memory.

When travel restrictions were lifted, and we were once again able to fly, I had to relearn what before had been muscle memory. Packing took much longer, getting to the airport was more stressful, and just making my way from the curb, through security, and to the gate felt strange and unfamiliar. Most things hadn't changed. In fact, the whole travel experience was much as it had been two years before. But I was different. Two years of being homebound had made me more timid, less adventurous, unsure of myself. I had become more insular, less accustomed to seeing people in person, and more introverted.

While I'm confident that this is temporary, and that with time and exposure, I will once again venture confidently into the world and interact with people as I had before, I can't ignore the impact on my state of mind of being confined within a limited space. I'm also not the only one. What has this confinement and separation done to us as a species? How has it impacted our openness to new experiences and people? How far has it set us back in venturing outside our familiar environments and embracing different people? Have we lost our curiosity? Have we become afraid of the unfamiliar?

But the fear of the different and the unfamiliar didn't start with the pandemic. Many people haven't had the opportunity to travel the globe, see its wonders, and encounter different people or cultures. Spending lifetimes close to home it's possible to lose perspective. We might lock ourselves behind barricades, imagining strangers to be our enemies, and peering out the peephole in terror for our lives. But it doesn't have to be that way. Instead of closing our minds in fear, we might instead choose to step outside the garden gate to embrace the adventure that beckons where the path winds out of view.

Chapter 61

The Return of Spontaneity

September 2

> *When we feel down, a simple act of creation can sometimes lift us up again - writing, drawing, something, fixing, cleaning, or whatever else moves us. There is satisfaction in the doing and in gazing at what we've accomplished. Find something small to create and embark on a better, happier day.*

Some people like to plan things out, while others prefer to leave things open and take advantage of opportunities as they arise. For the past two years, we have been forced into a strange duality, in which we had to plan better than before while knowing that our plans might be dashed by some new development of the pandemic, and that we'll have to act spontaneously anyway.

Pre-pandemic, we could decide what to eat at the last minute, running to the store, ordering takeout, or going out. During the lockdown, we went shopping less frequently, bought what we could, and planned out each meal in advance. Our meals became predictable and repetitive, and the rest of our lives followed suit. We stayed home, picked up hobbies, and got comfortable doing less, with each day resembling the one before.

At the same time, we learned to improvise, when our stores ran out of hand soap and toilet paper, or when we were first told to wash and then not to wash our groceries. We had to rethink holidays and social events, weddings were postponed or muted, and we had to learn how to be virtual, attending meetings with small children hanging from our necks or animals walking across the desk. We were like small boats moored in the harbor, going nowhere but still knocked about by the waves.

As the pandemic receded into the background of our minds, life started returning to normal. Likewise, we are seeing the return of spontaneity, real spontaneity, driven by whim and desire rather than by reaction to unforeseeable events. Some of us are choosing to engage in last-minute travel, enticed by low-cost airfares and driven by cabin fever after being confined to our homes and neighborhoods for far too long. Others are inviting people for dinner, going to concerts, or grabbing a drink at a local tavern after a long day. Like children at recess, released from classes and obligations, we've begun to run around and explore.

We are a curious and opportunistic species, and the ability to act on a momentary impulse is very healthy for us. Only now, after being restricted and confined, can we appreciate the impact of spontaneity on our physical and mental health. Sometimes, we only notice how important something is to us after it is taken away for a while. I'm glad for the return of spontaneity but also wonder what else we're taking for granted, and what it will take to make us notice and appreciate what we have.

Chapter 62

Back to Normal

September 22

> *Virtues, taken to extreme, can turn into vices. Frugal becomes cheap, detail-oriented, becomes perfectionist, helpful becomes overbearing. Let us be vigilant lest our virtues lose their virtue.*

September has arrived, and with it a return to our normal, pre-pandemic lives. Schools have reopened, people are back at work, and it feels like the difficulties of 2020 and 2021 are now behind us. Governments have declared that the pandemic is over, testing and vaccination rates are diminishing, and our attitude about Covid-19 is shifting from fear to acceptance. Sure, we might get sick, but it's more of an inconvenience, like a cold or flu, than a deadly disease.

While infections are mostly confined to the elderly or immunocompromised, getting infected is still dangerous, so people are still getting hospitalized and dying from the disease. In his 1929 novel, *All Quiet on the Western Front,* Erich Maria Remarque tells the story of a soldier, Paul Bäumer, who is killed on an exceptionally quiet day of the war, and no one notes his suffering or death. We must still care for those who fall ill, are impacted by long Covid or whose lives are disrupted because they or people under their care have tested positive.

So, as we embrace the return to normalcy, we should reach out to those for whom not everything is normal. If we are healthy, and all of those around us are fine, it's easy to forget that some other people might not be. The pandemic left many scars, physical and emotional, and many people missing loved ones who didn't make it. By enlarging our perspective as we return to normal, we can bring more of us along, support those still struggling, and honor those we lost along the way.

The legacy of Covid-19 can be increased kindness, empathy, and caring among its survivors, paving the way to happier times ahead. While we crave a return to normalcy, we also have an opportunity to create a new normal that improves upon our pre-pandemic state and builds a better future. We can reimagine our work and home lives, balancing our personals and professional lives in a more harmonious manner. We can lead more fulfilling lives while being more productive and spend more time working and less time getting to and from our offices. We can bond and socialize while also optimizing our quiet working time, and we can approach old problems with new solutions.

Our new normal will begin to feel normal, after a while, even as it differs from our pre-pandemic state. The more intentional we are, and the more we act to ensure to bring as many of the people around us along on the journey, the more likely we are to enjoy our new normal, whatever form it takes.

Chapter 63

Pessimism is a Luxury

September 27

> *Optimism needs to be our choice because all our other choices are worse and because, sometimes, it may be all we've got.*

It's been said that optimism is a luxury afforded the privileged few while the rest of humanity toils under the hot sun, barely catching its breath. It's easier to feel hopeful when we have the time and resources to think about the future and looking for the positives in everything can only happen when we are suffering. By those definitions, optimism is indeed a luxury.

Another view of optimism is the lemons out of lemonade idea – making the most of whatever life throws at us. I learned this type of optimism from my grandmother, who, fighting cancer, was no longer able to walk, so she learned how to knit. Unable to hold down food, she would still go to restaurants just for the outing and companionship. In the last year of her life, the most basic bodily functions became a struggle, but her quality of life was the highest it could have been.

Viktor Frankl said that "Everything can be taken from a man but one thing: the last of the human freedoms—to choose one's attitude in any given set of circumstances, to choose one's own way." "When we are no longer able to change a situation, we are challenged to change ourselves." He said this despite spending three years in concentration camps where his father died of starvation and pneumonia, his mother and brother were murdered in the gas chambers, and his wife died of typhus.

Optimism, resilience, and grit are therefore inextricably linked, allowing us to push past adversity and salvage the best outcomes from difficult circumstances. Without them, we wallow in anger, blame, and self-pity. Pessimism is therefore the luxury, and too often, we indulge in negative thinking to our own detriment and that of those around us. Life can be very hard, and pain is real. Optimism doesn't make the awful parts of reality go away, nor does it make them less difficult, but it does give us something to hold onto as we muddle through.

When we allow ourselves to be pessimistic, we become wrapped up in ourselves, unable to give to those around us. We infect others with our negativity and spread hopelessness and fear. We can only do this when society can function without us or when others can be positive despite our influence. History shows that when pessimism takes over, the result is often misery and death, not only for ourselves, but for many others as well.

We don't know what tomorrow will bring, but it's fair to assume that, like today, it will be a mix of good and bad, challenges and opportunities. There will always be shadows in our world, but we mustn't miss their striking beauty nor forget the brilliant sunshine that created them nor. Every day, the universe makes its move, and the next move is up to us. Like optimism, pessimism is also a choice, just not a good one.

Chapter 64

Endings

October 2

> *There comes a time to call it quits for the day, even if the pile of work is still high and the list of tasks is far from complete. After all, tomorrow is another day - we must disconnect and recharge, to face the new day's challenges with full energy and vigor.*

All things end, making room for new, and sometimes better futures in their wake, but while we know this in our minds, our hearts fight ferociously to deny, delay, or alter the inevitable. It is normal to feel nostalgic or sad when we contemplate endings and natural to try and hold onto the comfortable and familiar. Change often involves immediate and painful losses even if it results in better outcomes down the road.

Our lives involve a series of endings. We are born and may enjoy a few years of innocence before the realities of adulthood encroach and overtake us. We graduate from preschool, kindergarten, primary school, middle school, and high school, with each rite of passage marking an ending and transition. Throughout our lives, we encounter other endings, some routine, such as changing jobs or moving houses, and some wrenching, like the loss of friends or loved ones. The river of time only flows in one direction, and as it sweeps us along, different points on the riverbank come into view only to disappear around the next bend.

Some of the most difficult endings involve decisions, in which it is up to us to end what we are doing now and to choose a different path. Sometimes the choices are easy or obvious, but at other times, the upsides and downsides of different paths are less clear. In those cases, while keeping things as they are might feel like the less risky choice, we still need the courage to end things and move on. Our hand might hesitate as it reaches for the door, knowing that once we step through and close it, there might be no way back, but if we falter and turn away rather than go through, we are diminished.

Anxiety makes it harder to face these difficult choices, be they related to our careers, personal relationships, business ventures, pastimes, or anything else. We look both ways, analyze situations repeatedly, and even when we know the best path ahead, linger till time chooses for us. But, in the end, a door closes behind us whether we walk through it willingly or are pushed by the hand of time. One way or another, life goes on. We therefore need to accept and embrace endings even as they make us uncomfortable.

When we first went into lockdown, in March of 2020, I started writing weekly articles just like this one, and sharing them in my social media. Now, two and half years and 125 articles later, it's time to move on. I've enjoyed sharing my thoughts and ideas with you and am grateful that you've travelled alongside me on this journey through the pandemic. I still hope to continue the conversation, but in other ways. Alas, an ending, and while I feel wistful already, I also know that it's the right choice. I hope my words inspired your thinking and brought you comfort and joy. Thank you for joining me.

Concluding Thoughts

I hope you enjoyed and got value out of the ideas I shared in this second volume of essays. As with the first volume, perhaps some made you smile, or think, or do something differently than before. Now that this pandemic diary has reached its conclusion, we can either try to forget all about the last three years and attempt to recreate what we had before, or we can learn lessons about the world and about ourselves and create an even better future.

In my mind, we can only go forward, not back, and we have an awesome opportunity to shape our reality. The ideas I've shared with you are just one person's musings, but hopefully they'll start a conversation in which we all pool our creativity and thought together. I look forward to exchanging opinions, arguing, debating, and tackling the world's challenges together.

I know that, once in a while, I'll keep coming back to review my writing from this unprecedented time. Looking back at my words from this period will hopefully help me be more reflective, more thoughtful, more purposeful in my actions, while also giving me comfort and making me smile. I hope my musings help you as well and accompany you on your own journey forward.

Moshe

Index

Optimism and Positive Thinking

1: The Optimistic Pessimist, 12
6: Not All Bad, 22
11: What Are We Made Of?, 32
20: Beyond Alternative Facts, 50
26: Angry, 62
29: The Day After, 68
32: Beyond the Red Giant, 74
44: Optimism and the End of Humanity, 98
53: The Tides, 116
59: The Sandcastle, 128
62: Back to Normal, 134
63: Pessimism is a Luxury, 136

Choices and Mindfulness

1: The Optimistic Pessimist, 12
3: People are Annoying!, 16
5: Choices, 20
6: Not All Bad, 22
7: Angry Earth, 24
8: Summer Infestations, 26
9: Ordinary Extraordinary, 28
10: Worlds Gone By, 30
11: What Are We Made Of?, 32
12: Irrational Fears, 34
13: The Year of the Introvert, 36
14: Lest We Forget, 38
15: The Meaning of Life, 40
17: Everything is Temporary, 44

18: Out of Control, 46
19: Time is Finite, 48
22: Bummer, Bumper, Bumpy, 54
23: No Plans or Goals, 56
24: Comfort in the Mundane, 58
25: Learning Greek, 60
26: Angry, 62
27: The Small Stuff, 64
29: The Day After, 68
31: Nothing is Real, 72
32: Beyond the Red Giant, 74
33: Hot and Cold, 76
35: Moving On, 80
36: The Great Reset, 82
37: Invisible Anxiety, 84
38: Henchmen, 86
42: Yes or No?, 94
45: What Do We Know?, 100
46: The Passage of Time, 102
47: Never Good Enough, 104
48: Where to Begin, 106
49: Ripples, 108
50: A Quiet Day, 110
51: Money, 112
52: Up, Up and Away, 114
55: The Bystander Effect, 120
57: Feeling the Heat, 124
59: The Sandcastle, 128
61: The Return of Spontaneity, 132
63: Pessimism is a Luxury, 136
64: Endings, 138

Gratitude and Humility

2: A Whale Story, 14
6: Not All Bad, 22
9: Ordinary Extraordinary, 28

Empathy

    3: People are Annoying!, 16
    21: Outrage and Empathy, 52
    37: Invisible Anxiety, 84
    54: Not So Simple, 118
    62: Back to Normal, 134

Perspectives and Beliefs

2: A Whale Story, 14
4: Alone, but Okay with It, 18
6: Not All Bad, 22
7: Angry Earth, 24
10: Worlds Gone By, 30
16: When Will It End?, 42
17: Everything is Temporary, 44
20: Beyond Alternative Facts, 50
21: Outrage and Empathy, 52
22: Bummer, Bumper, Bumpy, 54
23: No Plans or Goals, 56
24: Comfort in the Mundane, 58
25: Learning Greek, 60
28: De-Graded, 66
29: The Day After, 68
30: Done with Covid, 70
31: Nothing is Real, 72
32: Beyond the Red Giant, 74
34: The Blizzard of 2022, 78
35: Moving On, 80
38: Henchmen, 86
39: Cousins, 88
40: The Rear-View Mirror, 90
41: Normal but Weird, 92
43: Inflation, 96
44: Optimism and the End of Humanity, 98
45: What Do We Know?, 100
46: The Passage of Time, 102

47: Never Good Enough, 104
50: A Quiet Day, 110
52: Up, Up and Away, 114
53: The Tides, 116
55: The Bystander Effect, 120
56: Lies and Illusions, 122
57: Feeling the Heat, 124
60: Go Away!, 130
62: Back to Normal, 134

Pandemic

3: People are Annoying!, 16
4: Alone, but Okay with It, 18
6: Not All Bad, 22
8: Summer Infestations, 26
12: Irrational Fears, 34
13: The Year of the Introvert, 36
14: Lest We Forget, 38
16: When Will It End?, 42
25: Learning Greek, 60
27: The Small Stuff, 64
30: Done with Covid, 70
36: The Great Reset, 82
41: Normal but Weird, 92
52: Up, Up and Away, 114
54: Not So Simple, 116
60: Go Away!, 130
61: The Return of Spontaneity, 132
62: Back to Normal, 134

Negotiation, Conflict, and Self-Advocacy

42: Yes or No?, 94
51: Money, 112
58: Always Negotiating, 126

Humor

2: A Whale Story, 14
8: Summer Infestations, 26
25: Learning Greek, 60

www.ingramcontent.com/pod-product-compliance
Lightning Source LLC
Chambersburg PA
CBHW071245070526
44583CB00017B/2332